Praying THE EUCHARIST

Reflections on the
Eucharistic Experience of God

Praying

THE
EUCHARIST

**Reflections on the
Eucharistic Experience of God**

Charles Miller

MOREHOUSE PUBLISHING

First published in Great Britain 1995
Society for Promoting Christian Knowledge

First American edition published by
Morehouse Publishing

Editorial Office
871 Ethan Allen Highway
Ridgefield, CT 06877

Corporate Office
P.O. Box 1321
Harrisburg, PA 17105

ACKNOWLEDGEMENTS

Quotations from *The Revised Standard Version of the Bible*,
copyright 1946, 1952, 1971 by the Division of Christian
Education of the National Council of the Churches of Christ
in the USA.

Quotations from *The New Revised Standard Version of the Bible*,
copyright 1989 (as above).

Book of Common Prayer adapted for *The Alternative Service
Book 1980*, copyright © The Central Board of Finance of the
Church of England.

A catalog record for this book is available from the Library of Congress.

ISBN 0-8192-1670-4

Printed in the United States of America

In memory of
Mother Ruth
and in thanksgiving for her
Sisters of the Community of the Holy Spirit
among whom I first learned to
love the Liturgy

Contents

Preface

What does it mean to pray the eucharist? That is the
simple yet important question to which this book seeks
to respond. The past several decades have witnessed
radical changes in the patterns and style of eucharistic
worship – *the* liturgy, as the universal Christian tradition
calls it – and more recently has come an unexpected but
remarkable growth of interest in spirituality. But so often
those two developments seem worlds apart. For a number of years, when my worship time was spent more on
the pew-side than on the altar-side, I have felt a persistent gap between our deep human potential for prayer
and our corporate worship at the eucharist. That sense
has transcended differences of churchmanship within
my own Anglican tradition and has crossed the wider
denominational boundaries as well.

We need, I have thought, to discover a viable eucharistic spirituality; to refashion our understanding and our
expectations of what praying at the eucharist means.
This book, therefore, seeks to pursue that task: to ex-
plore how we can experience the eucharist as an act of
prayer. It does so in a way which conforms to the different shape and emphases in contemporary eucharistic
worship, and with an avowed desire to draw upon the
rich heritage of the universal Christian tradition. Its
focus is the eucharist of contemporary Anglicanism as I
know it both in the United States and in England. But in
so far as Anglicanism's tradition of worship has from its

beginning been eclectic and, as we would put it today, ecumenical, that same breadth of Christian spiritual wisdom has been enlisted into these reflections. As such it is a small step toward creating a synthesis in traditions, perspectives and experiences which have often been needlessly kept apart.

The pages that follow are not a 'how to' about the eucharist, nor a devotional manual, although the quotations at the end of each chapter may be useful for meditations before the eucharist. Rather, it is a kind of conversation in which one practitioner of eucharistic worship, namely the author, engages the worship tradition of which he is a part to hear anew its message, to feed more satisfyingly upon what St Basil called its 'everlasting delights'. It is a conversation which others too may profitably share in as they seek to draw nearer to God at their church's eucharist Sunday by Sunday.

The Vicarage
New Marston, Oxford

Acknowledgements

The substance of these reflections developed over a number of years and I am indebted to the numerous groups and congregations in the city of Oxford and in the University's colleges who provided me – often unwittingly – with opportunities to consider the theme. I must express gratitude to my own college, Keble, where these thoughts were developed in chapel sermons, to the Sisters of the Love of God to whose Novitiate they were first delivered in something like their present form, and to those who read and commented upon the manuscript: Dr Marjorie Reeves, Barbara Oster, The Rev. Randall Haycock and Canon A. M. Allchin. I am much indebted to the congregation of St Michael and All Angels, New Marston, who have patiently been experimented upon as we have sought to put the import of these reflections into practice. Above all I wish to thank my wife Judith for her unflagging confidence in this effort.

Introduction

In what sense are we to understand the Christian liturgy, the eucharist, as an experience of God? The eucharist, Christians believe, is an encounter with the living God, a personal God, and so, like all personal encounters, it has a particular form. Indeed, the form of that encounter shapes the quality and at times even the possibility of such a meeting. We are surely right to affirm the presence of God everywhere. 'All this worlde, is, as it were, the temple of his DEITIE, consecrated to His worship, sanctified by His presence, and filled with His glorie,' a Scottish Anglican divine of the seventeenth century reminded his hearers under the inspiration of Isaiah 6.3.[1]

Yet that very truth arises out of the belief that there are particular places and covenanted ways in which God lovingly commits himself to meet us. We believe this about Jesus himself and that is why he is for us not simply Jesus of Nazareth but Jesus *Christ*, the Messiah, the Anointed One, the Saviour. Whereas there have been and will be countless testimonies to what God is like, how he relates to us and how we relate to him, Jesus is *Christ* and *Saviour* for us because we believe that in him the divine–human encounter has acquired an absolute form. Therefore today people speak of Jesus himself as *the* sacrament of the presence of God. In him the 'Great Encounter' takes place.[2]

The astonishing basis of the Christian life is that we are called by baptism to live in Jesus Christ so that we might share his life with the Father. Yet this life in Christ by which we live for the Father is not something merely notional or emotional. From the time of the first Christians it was recognized that life in Christ has at its centre the celebration of the eucharist, what the writer of the Acts of the Apostles seems to refer to when he speaks of the apostolic teaching and fellowship, the breaking of bread and the prayers (Acts 2.42). There is the supreme covenanted occasion of our encounter with God because that celebration seeks to nurture the deepest fellowship between the God of heaven and earth and each one of us.

What follows is a series of reflections on the eucharist and its relation to that encounter with God which we call prayer. As 'reflections' they are necessarily tentative; they are stylistically various – sometimes more sermonic and meditational, sometimes more prosaic or scholarly – and they depend on my own admittedly personal experience and consideration of the church's tradition of eucharistic worship. But sometimes the thoughts which seem most personal and unique to oneself are in fact the very ones most widely held or felt. A seemingly personal view can be the handmaid of a truly catholic sensibility. The reader must judge whether in this case it is so.

The task, then, is to repossess an awareness of the possibilities of encounter with God through the eucharist. It will involve consideration of the basic structure of the eucharist. My purpose, though, is not to dwell on the factual and developmental details which other writers have covered so well nor to provide a manual or 'how to' for the parish communion.[3] Instead I want to consider the form, content and manner of celebrating the eucharist in light of the encounter with God in prayer which is its rationale and end. In other words, these reflections attempt to relate considerations of the shape and content of the eucharist to an interpretation

of their significance as a means for meeting God in
prayer.

Why embark upon such a task? For over a decade and
a half women and men have felt ever more acutely the
need to acknowledge and satisfy a long-ignored spiritual
hunger. In 1970 Jacques Ellul rendered his verdict that
'the man of our times does not know how to pray; but
much more than that, he has neither the desire nor the
need to do so'.[4] Now his words seem wildly out of date.
For Christians, as for so many others, spirituality is 'in'.
But for Christians, as for anyone else, the dangers of a
rampant groping for a spiritual life – however it may be
defined – are many, not least a lack of sound discrimi-
nation among those whose spiritual hunger outstrips
their spiritual discernment. 'In the absence of genuine
nourishment,' we have been reminded, 'the human spirit is forced to feed on any scraps it can find.'[5] Christians,
even those committed to a traditional pattern of liturgical worship, may become scavengers in their search for
soul food. It is unfortunate, therefore, that the desire to
encounter God through various forms of spirituality has
not included as a matter of course nor as a necessary
foundation the celebration of the eucharist. Is it because
people find it difficult to discern and experience the
prayer dimension of the eucharist? Is it because its
prayer potential has been lost sight of or inadvertently
smothered by other needs or priorities? However that
may be, these reflections seek to bridge the gap. Their
purpose is to help contemporary Christians experience
the eucharist in the same way our Christian forebears
did, as the school of prayer.

Taking up the theme of encounter, one of the spiritual masters of our century has written thus:

As from the beginning, we are in the presence of our
God. As in the time of Christ, we stand face to face

with a God who willed to become man and, as of old, day in and day out, human beings meet face to face in a completely new way once they have recognized in Jesus of Nazareth the Son of God and through him have seen the Father. This encounter takes place all the time, but our awareness is so dim that we miss its significance, its immeasurable possibilities and also what it claims from us.[6]

In many ways those words capture the motive for what follows. As the occasion of a covenanted experience of that 'Great Encounter' in Jesus Christ, the church's celebration of the eucharist invites us into that encounter by prayer. But so often its significance, its possibilities for prayer elude us. Therefore we must learn anew how it offers us opportunities for engagement with God. We must learn how to converse with God not by considering abstractly how it might or ought to happen, nor by presuming that it simply does happen. Rather, we must enter sensitively into the context of ongoing engagement with God where the etiquette of divine–human conversation and exchange is learned and taken up by each of us as we too join the dialogue with our divine Host.

1
Beginning the Journey

Over the entrance to the chapel which deacon Nicholas
Ferrar and his community erected at Little Gidding in
Huntingdonshire in the early seventeenth century are
inscribed words from the Book of Genesis: 'This is none
other than the House of God and the gate of heaven'
(Gen. 28.17). In the years before the English Civil War
their chapel was widely known as a place of prayer and
a living testimony to a rediscovery of sacramental worship and eucharistic prayer as embodied in the *Book of
Common Prayer*. The inscription is significant. It speaks
on the one hand of a 'house', a dwelling, a place of abid-
ing, of conversation and encounter. On the other hand
it speaks of a 'gate' which is passed through, an entry, a
place of passage, of pilgrimage, of journeying into God.
Both of those themes are central to the experience of
the eucharist: it is at once an occasion, a place of
encounter *with* God, and an event of pilgrimage *toward*
God. It is an occasion of encounter because it is the gate-
way of a spiritual journey.

Those words from Genesis inscribed upon the chapel
at Little Gidding suggest that prayer, and not least the
prayer of the church's eucharist, is a journey-like thing,
the occasion of a real spiritual movement. It contains too
an implicit awareness that prayer is not so much a defin-
able act as a movement toward a larger vision of reality,
an 'engodded' vision, to use a seventeenth-century word.

That we should regard prayer, even liturgical prayer,

in this way need not strike us as odd. Remember that
from its beginning as a movement Christianity was
described as 'the Way' (Acts 19.9). Christian prayer itself
also came to be described thus. There is a story of a
fourth-century monk from the Egyptian desert who was
told of a female recluse during his sojourn in Rome. She
lived, he was told, in one small room and she never went
out. The monk was sceptical about such a way of life, so
when he called upon the woman he asked her: 'Why are
you sitting here?' She replied: 'I am not sitting here. I am
on a journey.'[1] The journey theme reappears continually
in the Christian spiritual tradition. In his *Christian
Ethiks*, for instance, the Anglican priest–poet Thomas
Traherne encourages his reader 'to Travel'.[2] He refers, of
course, to the spiritual life. To pray is to embark upon a
journey toward God as he is made known in Jesus Christ.
To be a pray-er is to be a pilgrim.

Is it not fitting, then, to take up the journey theme in
regard to praying the eucharist? Admittedly, it is proba-
bly not a view of the eucharist which is foremost in our
minds. For a long time Christians have thought of the
eucharist as a thing, namely, 'the sacrament'; or as a
means of grace. As a result we have often ceased to see
it as an act or activity, a coming together to *do* and to
become something new and different. If, then, the door
of the church is likened to 'the gate of heaven', then
the liturgy itself is the form which the journey takes.

In fact, the opening words of the eucharist in the
American *Book of Common Prayer*, adapting a phrase
from the Byzantine liturgy, recall this theme of a
eucharistic journey: 'Blessed be God: Father, Son and
Holy Spirit. And blessed be his kingdom, now and for
ever. Amen.' That initial blessing of God, or doxology,
reminds us that the eucharist we celebrate is a journey
into the kingdom of God. The words of a prominent
Orthodox writer, who knows the significance of that

doxology out of a deep experience of the worship tradition from which it comes, are to the point:

> From the beginning the destination is announced: the journey is to the Kingdom. This is where we are going – and not symbolically, but really. In the language of the Bible, which is *the* language of the Church, to bless the Kingdom is not simply to acclaim it. It is to declare it to be the goal, the end of all our desires and interests, of our whole life, the supreme and ultimate value of all that exists. To bless is to accept in love, and to move toward what is loved and accepted. The Church thus is the assembly, the gathering of those to whom the ultimate destination of life has been revealed and who have accepted it. This acceptance is expressed in the solemn answer to the doxology: Amen. It is indeed one. of the most important words in the world, for it expresses the agreement of the Church to follow Christ in His ascension to his Father, to make this ascension the destiny of man.

With the doxology and its 'Amen', he goes on, the journey into God has begun.[3] Thus our eucharistic prayer is, like all prayer, a spiritual journey into another dimension, the kingdom, where God is all in all.

So then, the end of our journey is God's kingdom and the form of our journey is the eucharist. But how are we to travel? Who will be our guide? Here we discover the significance of Jesus. According to St John, Jesus is 'the way' (John 14.6). By describing him that way St John claims a unique role for Jesus in any authentic knowledge and experience of God. Surely for Christians, therefore, Jesus Christ will have a special role in that prayer life which is the foundation of our knowledge and experience of God. This is so all the more with respect

to the prayer of the eucharist from which and toward
which our Christian prayer flows.

Jesus Christ and the Eucharist

For centuries those who wrote about the meaning of the
eucharist described it in what is called a christological
way. That is, they attached symbolic importance to this
or that aspect of the service by linking it with some
feature of the life of Christ as we read it in the Gospels.
Such an approach allowed, even encouraged, creative
and imaginative symbolic interpretations. Today many
of them strike us as quaint or fanciful, maybe even a
hindrance to the 'real meaning' of the eucharist. For all
that, however, we should not lose sight of the basic
truth to which such a symbolic approach to our worship
points: our experience of God at the eucharist is determined by Jesus Christ the 'pioneer' of our salvation
(Heb. 2.10; 12.2) who leads us to the Father and his
kingdom. Our experience of God in the eucharist, as in
every other way, is determined by Jesus and his relationship to God.

Who is Jesus? What is his significance? The meaning
of Jesus is, of course, at the heart of Christian thinking
about God, the world and ourselves. St John's description of Jesus as 'the way' to the Father is taken here as
the basic theme by which we are to understand his role
in our eucharistic praying. The eucharistic experience of
God is therefore to be understood in the light of that
going to the Father (John 14.12) by means of which, St
John tells us, Jesus' mission is fulfilled and our reconcil-
iation to God accomplished.

To highlight Jesus' importance in the prayer of the
eucharist in this way is, at the same time, to draw
attention to the trinitarian character of our experience
of God at the eucharist. To speak of Jesus as the way is,

more particularly, to regard him as 'the way to the Father along which we are empowered to travel by the Holy Spirit'.[4] Rather than regard him as an isolated saviour or merely as an inspiring human example or, indeed, as our sacramental food, we must see him in the dynamic saving partnership of the triune God, Father, Son and Holy Spirit, into whose kingdom he leads us. If the Father is our destination and the Son our way, then it is the Holy Spirit who empowers us to travel.

Is that not part of the meaning of the so-called Collect for Purity with which the Anglican eucharist has always begun? Notice how it emphasizes the Spirit's work in enabling us to go to the Father through Jesus Christ:

> Almighty God, to whom all hearts are open, all desires known, and from whom no secrets are hidden: cleanse the thoughts of our hearts by the inspiration of your Holy Spirit, that we may perfectly love you, and worthily magnify your holy name; through Christ our Lord.[5]

And so the journey begins. Its form is the eucharistic liturgy itself. The Father is its end, the Spirit its energizing power, and Jesus Christ himself is the way.

Where is your journey, if not to the Lord God, to him whom we must love with all our heart, and with all our soul, and with all our mind?

St Augustine of Hippo

There is the head, here is the body; since nothing separates the head from its body. For if they were separated there would be no head and no body.

St John Chrysostom

Set this down, then: Christianity is a meeting.

Lancelot Andrewes

Come, all whoe'er have set
Your faces Zion-ward,
In Jesus let us meet,
and praise our common Lord:
In Jesus let us still go on,
Till all appear before His throne.

Nearer, and nearer still,
We to our country come,
To that celestial hill,
The weary pilgrim's home:
The new Jerusalem above,
The seat of everlasting love.

Our brother, Saviour, Head
Our all in all is He;
And in His steps who tread
We soon His face shall see;
Shall see Him with our glorious friends,
And then in heaven our journey ends.

Charles Wesley

It is a main enterprise for every individual to find the way
back to his heart.

Andre Louf

The Son becomes man in order to be the model and the cen-
tre from which a force shines out making men like Christ in
their striving towards God the Father. This force, which
becomes an intimate principle within all who believe yet
always remains at the same time above them, is the third
divine person, the Holy Spirit.

Dumitru Staniloae

2

The Prayer-shape of the Liturgy

To speak of the eucharistic journey as the previous chapter has done might suggest that it is a human act arising from a human impulse. That, however, is not the case since our experience of God at the eucharist should be understood within the basic pattern of encounter between God and humankind. The Byzantine liturgy expresses this truth succinctly when, at the beginning of the service, the deacon declares: 'It is time for the *Lord to act.*' Only after God acts can we act by way of response. The aim of this chapter is to describe the character of that experience of God's action and our response, and to see how the shape of prayer at the eucharist reflects it.

It is important to recall the christological basis of these reflections. They began by considering the eucharist as a journey dependent upon Jesus who is the way to the Father. But Jesus' significance for understanding eucharistic prayer is greater still since as the source of our joyful, trusting approach to God the Father he is also the pattern of our approach to God in prayer.

Jesus' connection with our prayer can be understood in many ways. Most often, perhaps, we think of him as the great teacher about prayer, as the one who has instructed us in the foundational prayer of all Christians,

11

the Lord's Prayer (Matt. 9.9–13; Luke 11.2–4). That new and radical prayer was Jesus' response to the disciples' request that Jesus teach them to pray. It reminds us that Jesus' significance for them as well as for us is in part that he teaches us how to pray.

But the Lord's Prayer does not stand in isolation as Jesus' single teaching on prayer. Rather, it is a bringing together of the themes which reappear throughout the Gospels' picture of the praying Jesus (to use Michael Ramsey's phrase).[1] A point which Michael Ramsey makes is significant here: for guidance in how to pray, Christians must look not just to the specific prayer which Jesus taught but to Jesus himself as a living expression of what it means to pray.

How then did Jesus pray? There is no doubt that the particular themes which characterize Jesus' prayer are central to the prayer of all believers: Father, kingdom, the divine will, to name but a few.[2] I prefer, however, to start at an even more basic level. Jesus was a Jew, and he prayed and taught others to pray according to the long-established tradition of Jewish prayer. Jesus' own prayer, in keeping with the character of Jewish prayer as a whole, is shaped by the Old Testament experience of God.[3] At the root of Jewish prayer is the experience of a God who acts in history. Those acts are a personal communication, an *enacted word* to those whom he calls into covenant relationship. (In Hebrew 'word' and 'act' are the same word: *dabar.*) In the Old Testament, therefore, the 'word of God' signifies those concrete actions of God in history by which he seeks a response of faith and love from humanity. God speaks or acts, humanity responds.

The call of Abraham, when God calls and Abraham responds in faith, sets the pattern of the whole subsequent relationship between God and his people (Gen. 12.1, 4). But it is in the story of Moses and the formation

of God's holy people in the giving of the Law that the
pattern is clear. After the Israelites had been led out of
Egypt the Lord, speaking through Moses, calls the
people together on Mount Horeb (Sinai) to make of
them his holy people (Exod. 19–20).[4] Several features of
the event are worth noting. First, the people are sum-
moned together by the word of God spoken through
Moses, and are gathered in order to hear that word.
Notice too that the word they hear is chiefly a recollec-
tion of God's saving deeds done on behalf of his people.
The word, therefore, is at the same time a deed; it
expresses the saving *acts* of God. Notice how the proclamation of that word evokes a response from the people:
' "Everything that the Lord has spoken we will do" '
(Exod. 19.8). It is a response of faithfulness, of gratitude,
of obedience to the word that has been proclaimed.
Lastly, by their obedient response to the word proclaimed, the Israelites become God's holy people: ' "Now
therefore, if you obey my voice and keep my covenant . . .
you shall be a priestly kingdom and a holy nation" '
(Exod. 19.5–6). Out of that relationship between God
and Israel came the distinctive shape of Jewish prayer.
Its foundation is the interaction between the word proclaimed and the human response given in return.[5]

The Praying Jesus

As the word and act of God to us, and as a man who
lived the human response to God perfectly, Jesus himself
embodies that pattern of interaction described above. In
him proclamation and response are one. His proclamation of God's word and his own response to it are
inseparable. That is why his conversation with God and
about God are drenched in the scriptures of the Old
Testament, their words, themes, images and prophecies.
How often Jesus responds to questions and situations

with the very words of the scriptures, as the episode of
Jesus' temptation shows (Matt. 4.1–11). He lives in the
word of God and his life, his being, is wholly responsive
to it. Jesus *is* the perfect prayer.

What is the importance of the pattern of proclamation and response, and Jesus' embodiment of it, for our
eucharistic prayer? An answer might begin with St Paul's
description of Christians as the 'body of Christ' (e.g. 1
Cor. 12.27). Our Christian forebears took this language
very seriously indeed, so much so that great theologians
such as St John Chrysostom and St Augustine spoke of
the members of the church as a real extension of the
humanity of Christ. The point is this: the ways of the
praying Jesus are likewise the ways of his praying body,
the church, and nowhere is this more so than at the
eucharist when in a unique way Jesus the head and we
his body are joined together through word, sacrament
and symbol. It is not surprising, then, that the church's
prayer at the eucharist reflects that pattern of proclamation and response. That pattern is, in fact, the means
by which we are led on our eucharistic journey. That
prayer-shape, as I call it, is a key element in our prayerful approach to God which the eucharist seeks to enable.

Equally, that prayer-shape offers a pattern by which
we can understand the overall structure of the liturgy as
an experience of prayer since it enables us to see the
relation between the various parts of the eucharist. Our
concern must not simply be 'this is the ancient pattern of
the Christian eucharist' but rather 'this is the pattern by
which we learn to pray like the praying Jesus; this is the
prayer-shape which can lead us to true conversation with
the God revealed in Jesus Christ.'

The Prayer-Shape of the Eucharist

To that end the arrangement of these reflections seeks to reorient the reader in terms of this basic prayer-shape, to provide a pattern according to which the eucharist's character as a continuous act of prayer can come more clearly into view. Its division into two main parts, 'Proclamation' and 'Response', indicates that the service of the Word and the service of the Sacrament (to use common but deceptive designations) reflect the twofold shape of proclamation and response. By this means I hope to highlight the biblical character of the church's eucharistic prayer and, in so doing, to provide a unified vision of the eucharist as an act of prayer.

It is still Jesus who teaches us to pray. But he does so now by his Holy Spirit through his eucharistic body, the church. The belief that the church really is the living body of Christ means that in its distinctive gathering at the eucharist the Lord still instructs us. More than that, in the eucharistic encounter with God we not only learn to pray as Jesus did, we actually pray with him too.

The liturgy has been to me a great theological teacher; a perpetual testimony that the Father, the Son and the Spirit, the one God blessed for ever, is the author of all life, freedom, unity to men; that our prayers are nothing but responses to His voice speaking to us and in us.

F. D. Maurice

Worship, in all its grades and kinds, is the response of the creature to the Eternal.

Evelyn Underhill

Christian prayer is response. In this it is distinguished from all those spiritual disciplines and exercises, however good, which are initiated by men and women for their own improvement, for their justification, for their own increase of self-control. The Christian says 'we love God because He first loved us'. Our love which ascends to God is the love which has come down from God.

Eric Abbott

3
Collective Prayer

The eucharistic journey is a journey of prayer. A guiding theme in these reflections is that our eucharistic prayer expresses the essential shape of prayer, namely, proclamation and response. Before going further, however, we should consider the prayer which concludes the preparatory part of the eucharist: the collect.

Years ago Evelyn Underhill reminded us of the tendency toward 'analysis and ordering of prayer' characteristic of our western Christian tradition. She contrasted it with the 'free spirituality and inwardness' of, for instance, the Orthodox experience of worship.[1] Her remark is a reminder that our western tradition of worship does lend itself to rather clear distinctions, and attributes specific forms and purposes to the various prayers included in the eucharist.

The collect prayer at the eucharist, so prominent in the Anglican Prayer Book tradition as well as in the Roman Catholic mass, readily falls within the scope of the ordered prayer of which Underhill spoke. From the early Christian era, through the time of Archbishop Thomas Cranmer's magisterial translations for England's reformed *Book of Common Prayer*, then into our own time, these succinct thematic prayers have been an important element in Christians' prayer at Sunday worship. It is typical of the collect prayer that it precedes the reading of Scripture; and as a standard genre of prayer it has come to have a distinctive form.[2] Through the beauty of their prose language and on account of their prominence in the simplified worship of the *Book of Common Prayer* the collects have assumed an important place in the spirituality nurtured by the tradition of Prayer Book worship.[3]

But as long as we speak of *the* collect we assume that the sum and substance of this act of prayer is the priest's praying of the collect. But in fact the collect itself is but a part of a larger act which I prefer to call 'collective prayer'[4] or 'collective praying'. To speak, as we customarily have done, of *the* collect suggests some*thing*, a single prayer, a specific formula of words spoken, in this case, by another person, to which the congregation gives in reply a ritual 'amen'. On the other hand, to speak of collective prayer or, better still, collective praying signifies an activity which involves the whole congregation. Collective praying is an inclusive event.

If we look at the form of collective praying from the evidence gleaned from the church's early worship it consists of four ingredients: first, an invitation to pray by the celebrant or president who leads the community's worship; second, a period of silent prayer offered by each member of the congregation; third, vocal or spoken prayer, namely, the given collect appointed for the occasion and offered by the priest; and fourth, a ratification of the prayers offered silently and aloud by the people's 'amen'. Although the praying of the collect has not reflected this dynamic character for centuries, nevertheless that fourfold pattern is still the paradigm and ideal of all collective prayer in public worship.[5]

The Privilege of Prayer

For centuries collective prayer began with an exchange between the president of the eucharist and the assembly:

'The Lord be with you.' 'And also with you.' Although brief and seemingly formulaic, that exchange is more meaningful than commonly supposed. The phrase is a translation of the older Latin exchange: *'Dominus vobiscum.'* *'Et cum spiritu tuo.'* What does that brief dialogue mean? First, it should be noticed that it declares the condition for the prayer act which follows. We are able to pray because of the prior work and presence of God who makes our prayer possible. The act of prayer is always set within the light of St Paul's humbling yet encouraging realization that 'we do not know how to pray as we ought, but the Spirit himself intercedes for us with sighs too deep for words' (Rom. 8.26). Our prayer, however feeble or eloquent, is possible by and in the presence of the Holy Spirit who as the giver of life enlivens our thoughts and words.

In addition, it is useful to realize that our long-standing English translation 'The Lord be with you' is only one possible translation of the Latin phrase from which it derives. We typically understand it as *'May* the Lord be with you' – a kind of wish or desire. But the phrase could easily be rendered as a simple matter of fact: 'The Lord *is* with you.' The formula still declares the condition of prayer but it is less a wish than a statement. Some contemporary versions of the eucharist use another translation of the Latin to make this very point: 'The Lord is here.' 'His Spirit is with us.'[6]

In fact the Christian life is such that both interpretations are apt. The first highlights the invocational character of the Christian experience, that is, the fact that in living our faith we must constantly call the power of the Spirit down upon ourselves not just to avoid what is sinful or destructive but equally to do what is good and upbuilding. The second understanding pointedly recalls the privilege of prayer that is given to Christians by their baptism. When we are bathed in Holy Spirit we are engrafted into Christ and become participants in his perpetual life of prayer, and so are able to pray in him. This important fact, hinted at as collective prayer begins, acquires greater significance both as collective prayer unfolds and also as the whole eucharistic journey advances. Our prayer in Christ, therefore, is a theme to which we will have reason to return elsewhere.

'Ask and Ye Shall Receive'

The Holy Spirit is present to us as the enabling Spirit of our prayer. The opening exchange with which collective prayer begins therefore leads naturally to an invitation to pray: 'Let us pray.' But what sort of prayer?

It has been pointed out that prayer in the New Testament can readily be described in terms of either asking or thanking.[7] That basic distinction applies to the prayers of the eucharist as well. In the case of asking, a further distinction can be made between asking for oneself, which we call petition or petitionary prayer, and asking on behalf of others, which we call intercession or intercessory prayer. Both are mentioned in the New Testament, and it is interesting to consider whether the reference to 'prayer, intercession and thanksgiving' (1 Tim. 2.1) does not reflect an early pattern of eucharistic worship. However that may be, the point here is that collective prayer is a form of petitionary prayer. The invitation 'Let us pray', therefore, bids each member of the congregation to offer petitions for him or herself.

One consequence of this experience of collective prayer is that it pays little heed to the distinction or opposition between liturgical or corporate prayer and private or personal prayer. The genuine bidding for individuals' petitionary prayer within the act of collective prayer as a whole is rooted in a spiritual world-view which knew no rigid distinction between corporate and private in the experience of prayer. But despite changes

in the language, tone and content of our worship we are
still far from achieving a proper complementarity
between the personal and the corporate aspects of
prayer.[8]

It is inadequate, therefore, to view our public, corporate prayer at, say, the eucharist as necessarily
impersonal, as an older approach to the liturgy did. All
liturgical prayer is in some sense incomplete until it
engages each one of us personally. 'Until this contact
has been established,' Louis Bouyer once insisted, 'there
is no prayer properly speaking.' He goes on to describe
the necessary parts played in prayer by the church as a
corporate body on the one hand and the individual on
the other. 'Without questions,' he says,

> this meeting with God is brought about in the Church,
> and for that matter, properly speaking, it is always the
> Church who is speaking, it is always the Church who
> is the interlocutor with God in the dialogue of prayer.
> But the Church as believing and loving, exists only in
> us . . . Here the task of each person is irreplaceable:
> no one can substitute for anyone else; the community,
> while transcendent to the individuals composing it,
> lives only by the grace in each of its members.[9]

So, the invitation to petitionary prayer, 'Let us pray', is
a summons to each member of the congregation to offer
prayers on his or her own behalf as we each exist in our
particular and unique circumstances. At the same time,
we pray as those whose individual situation before God
is entwined with the assembly of fellow believers, the
body of Christ, in relation to whom our own needs are
defined, qualified and fulfilled.

The Search for Silence

It is just this personal element in collective prayer that
accounts for the dimension of silence within the full

form of collective praying as it was originally practised.[10] The act of prayer was not the spoken prayer of the priest alone but a combination of silent and spoken elements in which the different orders present contributed in various ways.[11] Every occasion of collective prayer, therefore, included the silent or 'hushed' prayer offered by each person present followed by the vocal prayer of the president or celebrant.[12] This may seem strange since many people regard silent or interior prayer as out of place in corporate worship. But, in the ancient Christian understanding out of which this pattern arose, interior and vocal prayer were viewed as interrelated and mutually sustaining. And so, collective prayer calls for a 'fruitful interaction' between silent and vocal prayer.[13]

But the world of silence, that 'Holy Wilderness' as philosopher Max Picard once called it, is one in which we tread warily and uncomfortably. In our modern sound-cluttered world where silence is often no more than 'the momentary breakdown of noise' we come upon silence as upon a stranger.[14] There are, of course, many kinds of silence. In our worship it is important to regard silence not as something negative, not as an absence, but as something positive and pregnant. Speech and silence, Picard insisted, belong together because all speech, all conversation is interwoven with silence.[15] 'Real speech is the resonance of silence.'[16] There is no communication, no sentence, no word whose meaning is not dependent on silent spaces, however brief or subtle, which separate paragraph from paragraph, sentence from sentence, word from word, and sound from sound.

A prayerful encounter with God at the eucharist, therefore, is a dialogue woven out of the intermingling strands of silence and speech. The dialogue of liturgical prayer, like clouds in the sky, takes shape above a deep, eternal silence and stillness apart from which all attempts to speak to God and one another are but gibberish.

This awareness has not been lost on God's people. From Elijah's hearkening to the still, small voice (1 Kings 19.12), to the psalmist's urging to 'be still and know' (Ps. 46.11), to St Ignatius of Antioch's description of Jesus' becoming man as an event wrought 'in the silence of God',[17] the weaving of silence and speech as the clothing of our dialogue with God has been affirmed. Although the importance of silence has been recognized in the realm of private prayer, it has failed to make much of a mark in the eucharistic worship of the average Christian congregation. But collective praying will never be authentic until free silent prayer and formal vocal prayer are reunited.

What kind of silence is it? It is possible, for instance, to distinguish active silence from passive silence. An active silence signifies silence in which *we* are the chief speakers. It is distinguishable from passive silence in which we attend to *someone else* who is addressing us. Overall, the eucharist is meant to include both. But the silence in collective praying is best viewed as an active silence: it is given to us so that we can speak and offer our petitions to God. Thus, the silence of collective praying is not a silence of attentive, receptive waiting, but one where we ourselves actively contribute toward dialogue with God.

At the practical level it is difficult to think of any other way in which a group of people could effectively offer individual petitions at one and the same time. Through silent, interior prayer we are freed from the need for eloquence or precision, or the temptation to wordiness. Thank goodness that is so, since in the complexity of who we are with our many needs, wants, hurts and hopes, the spoken word can so easily fail:

Words strain,
Crack and sometimes break, under the burden,
Under the tension, slip, slide, perish,
Decay with imprecision, will not stay in place,
Will not stay still.[18]

If the silence of collective prayer deprives us of audible words it can for that very reason give wider scope for expression of the needs, wants and desires out of which petitionary prayer rises. St Gregory the Great spoke eloquently of the value of prayer that goes beyond, or rather beneath our words. For, he once explained,

> it is not our words that make the strongest impression on the ears of God, but the desires. Thus, if we seek eternal life with the mouth but do not readily desire it with the heart, when we cry we are really silent. But if we desire in the heart, even when our mouth is silent, in our silence we cry aloud. Thus it says in the Gospel: when you say your prayers, you must go into your private room, and shut the door, and say your prayers to your Father who is in secret. And your Father, who sees what is done in secret, will give you your reward in full. For when the door is shut, someone prays in his private room when, while his mouth is silent, he pours forth the affection of his heart in the sight of the heavenly pity. And the voice is heard in secret, when it cries out in silence with holy desires.[19]

So, in the silence of collective praying there is the possibility of discovering that quality of 'personal worship', 'free-spirituality' and 'inwardness' which our tradition of worship has sometimes lacked.[20]

The Praying Jesus, Head and Body

Collective prayer reaches its completion in the vocal prayer known as the collect. Although we are used to

hearing such prayers said or sung as the sum total of collective prayer, we can see now that the collect itself is the
completing thread in the fabric of this act of prayer. Its
'sober and pure' quality rooted in the corporate experience and wisdom of the tradition out of which it comes,
when joined to the very personal and free silent prayer,
makes for an authentic expression of the church at
prayer.[21]

The collect complements the private petitions of worshippers by drawing them together, by 'collecting' them
into one single petition which completes each expression
of personal need in light of the whole church's ceaseless
round of petition to God.[22] An important part of collective prayer, therefore, is the process by which an individual's momentary sense of needs and wants is nuanced,
qualified, perhaps even changed by the church's expression of what its members are called to pray for.[23]

In fact for the attentive worshipper the content of petitionary prayer can change under the influence of the
church's cycle of collects. Sometimes what one of us may
ask of God is singularly 'in tune' with what Christians at
large are asking for themselves on a particular occasion.
At other times our perceived needs are at variance.
Whereas the whole pattern of collective praying never
requires us to abandon our personal petitions to God, it
always calls us to place them within the perspective of
the kingdom which qualifies our own partial insights.

Beginning in the seventeenth century, those committed to a spirituality nourished by the *Book of Common
Prayer* made much of Cranmer's brilliant cycle of collects. Manuals of devotion saw in them the centre of the
Christian's prayers and meditations for each week of the
year. The familiarity it bred with the petitionary themes
of the collects is something an authentic eucharistic
spirituality must recover.[24]

But there is more still to the significance of the

collects. It is widely acknowledged by those who have
studied the collect's origins that its characteristic features
are its opening address to God (most often 'Almighty
God' in the *Book of Common Prayer*), and its conclusion
'through Jesus Christ our Lord'. The concluding phrase
is the more consequential of the two. The concept of
prayer 'through' Christ expresses Jesus' role as a mediator or go-between for God and humankind (Heb. 9.15).
In the New Testament, the Letter to the Hebrews, drenched in the liturgical imagery of the Old Testament,
develops the theme of Jesus as mediator between God
and humankind, and does so in connection with the idea
of intercession. 'He always lives', says the writer, 'to make
intercession for them' (7.25). Michael Ramsey reminded
us that the meaning of Jesus' perpetual intercession,
which the Letter to the Hebrews links with his role as
high priest and mediator, is at heart very simple: as Jesus
prayed on earth so he continues to pray in heaven.[25] His
intercession is the expression of his positive, confident
relationship of love toward both God and us. Ramsey
explained it this way:

> When we say 'he lives to make intercession' we note
> that the verb ἐντυγχάνειν [entugkhanein] which we
> habitually translate 'intercede' means literally not to
> make petitions or indeed to utter words at all but to
> *meet*, to *encounter*, to *be with* someone on behalf of or
> in relation to others. Jesus is *with* the Father; with him
> in the intimate response of perfect humanity; with
> him in the power of Calvary and Easter; with him as
> one who bears us all upon his heart, our Son of Man,
> our friend, our priest; with him as our own.[26]

As if to heighten the connection between our prayer
and Jesus' intercessory prayer as Hebrews understands
it, early Christian worshippers sometimes added to the
name of Jesus the phrase our 'high priest'.[27]

A similar view of the relationship between our prayer and Jesus' is found in the practice of praying 'in the name of' Jesus Christ. It is a phrase with which the collects customarily end. In the Acts of the Apostles Christians are known as those who invoke the name of Jesus (9.14). This aspect of our prayer is characteristic of St Paul and St John. For St Paul, prayer in the name of Jesus is a statement about the authority by which Christians pray. At the same time it signals dependence on the person in whose name we pray. Likewise for St John. As the climax of his Gospel approaches Jesus bids his disciples pray in his name while he also informs them that 'apart from me you can do nothing' (15.5). In both cases we depend upon the praying Jesus through whom our prayers are heard and accepted.[28]

It is hard for us to grasp the significance attached to a name in the Bible and the ancient world. For the Hebrew and Greek mind one's name was linked to one's identity in a profound way. Prayer in Jesus' name signalled, therefore, prayer deeply bound up with Jesus' unique identity, his power and his way of being. Thus prayer 'in the name of' Jesus or 'through' him expresses the intimacy between Christ and each believer which both gives life and enables prayer.

As for St Paul, so for us the meaning of prayer 'in the name of' Jesus is of a piece with the vision of Christian life 'in Christ'. Indeed Paul's language about prayer 'in the name of' Christ and Christian life 'in Christ' is part and parcel of his distinctive use of body language when describing the church. Collective prayer is closely tied to Paul's understanding of the church as 'the body of Christ', part of the glorified body of the risen Lord (see 1 Cor. 10.17).[29] As the one who draws all things into relation with God (Eph. 1.10) Christ is the 'head' of the new body of believers (Eph. 4.15). We regard these terms as metaphorical. Early Christians, however, viewed them as really, albeit spiritually, true. St Athanasius, for instance, built upon St Paul's perspective and actually identified Christians themselves with the very humanity of Christ.[30] Through that solidarity we have access to heaven.[31] St John Chrysostom, using images from worship, spoke of two altars, one made of stone, the sacramental one, and the other made of human persons, 'the very members of Christ'. And his contemporary St Augustine captured this whole strain of thought when he spoke of 'the whole Christ, head and body'.[32]

Collective prayer, then, is neither Jesus' prayer alone nor our prayer alone. It is a communion of prayer arising out of what the Anglican divine Richard Hooker called the 'marvellous conjunction' between Christ the head of the church and us his body.[33] His prayer is our prayer, and our prayer is his. In collective prayer we enact that exhortation made by the writer of the Letter to the Hebrews when he beckons his readers to 'draw near with a true heart in full assurance of faith' to the throne of the living God (Heb. 10.19, 22).

That spiritual relationship was expressed in the actual arrangement of the worshippers as they engaged in the collective prayer of the eucharist. The early Christians seem to have followed the pattern of the Jewish synagogue with which they were already familiar. There the rabbi, or teacher of the community, was seated amid the congregation with a council of elders around him facing the place where the sacred scrolls, the Torah, were kept. When Christians adopted this pattern, the celebrant of the eucharist sat in the place previously occupied by the rabbi. Around him gathered the elders, together with the deacons, and behind them the laity. Everyone faced the holy table at the east end of the room.[34] Everyone sat before the word of God as devout hearers. Everyone engaged in collective prayer according to their role, and the overall 'succession of actors'[35] meant that the gathering itself became an image of the whole Christ, head and body. The faithful, Christ's living body, offer their petitions; then their prayers are gathered up and completed by the head of the assembly who is an image of Christ the body's head as he presents our prayers to God by joining the people's prayers to his.[36]

Collective prayer thus reminds us that we always pray in intimate union with the praying Jesus. Equally, as it is performed, collective prayer is the first clear step in the 'embodying' by which the Holy Spirit recreates the spiritual union between Christ and the members of his body.

The invisible Christ is made present through and in the visible unity of the bishop and his people, the head and the body.

St Ignatius of Antioch

He prays for us, as our priest; He prays in us as our head; He is prayed to by us, as our God. Let us recognize then our words in Him, and His words in us.

St Augustine of Hippo

Doth any man doubt that even from the flesh of Christ our very bodies do receive that life which shall make them glorious at the latter day, and for which they are already counted parts of his blessed Body?

Richard Hooker

The very name of 'Head' hath the signification not only of dominion but of union; and therefore while we look upon him at the right hand of God, we see ourselves in heaven.

John Pearson

Christianity . . . is never solitary. It is never true to say that separate persons are united to Christ, and then combine to form the Church; for to believe in Christ is to believe in One whose Body is a part of Himself, and whose people are His own humanity, and to be joined to Christ is to be joined to Christ-in-His-Body; for 'so is Christ' and Christ is not otherwise.

Michael Ramsey

The heart of being, the blessed Trinity above all worlds, is not a mystery by which the knowledge of God is withheld from our enquiring minds. It is a pattern of life into which we ourselves, by an unspeakable mystery, are taken up. For Christ joins us with himself in the continual, practical, daily choice of his Father as our father. Why, he makes us part of himself, he calls us his members, his eyes and tongue, his hands and feet. He puts us where he is, in Sonship to his Father, and opens to us the inexhaustible and all-quickening fountain, the spirit of Sonship, the river of life, the Holy Ghost.

Austin Farrer

4

The Mystery of the Word: Proclamation

In Christian experience God takes the initiative in speaking to us. Our life of faith is but a response to God's gracious self-disclosure. In prayer the same is true: divine truth, God's presence, first opens itself to us; then we, in response, open our hearts and minds, our whole being, to it.[1] That pattern of divine–human encounter forms the central prayer-shape of the eucharist.

There are, of course, many approaches which we might take to grasp the character of our encounter with God at the eucharist. In so far as it is to be an engagement with God *in prayer*, the pattern of call or proclamation and response seems most fitting. But how is the pattern reflected in the service as it unfolds and in the arrangement of the present book? This chapter is concerned with the act of God that is primary, his act of calling, of first speaking to us, expressed in the first half of the eucharist which is often called the service or liturgy of the Word. Then, from chapter seven, our act of response is taken up, treating the main elements of the service which follow the service of the Word. These reflections are thus structured around the twofold pattern of our experience of God: he speaks, we respond. But within the service of the Word itself the twofold prayer-shape operates, and this and the two following chapters reflect upon how this is so.

The Power of the Word

'The tabernacle is the Church, in which Christ is served. The table is sacred Scripture, on which the loaves, the nourishment of souls, are placed.'[2] So wrote the twelfth-century monk Honorius of Autun. Although writing in an age which we commonly think of as dismissive of the Bible, Honorius' striking image, clearly reminiscent of the eucharist, reveals a thoroughly ancient Christian view of Scripture. For the fathers of the church, as for the first Christians themselves, their religion was a religion of the word. The word in question was not merely written and mute; it was a living, incarnate and glorified Word personally active and ever in search of encounter with humanity now, as then, and until the end of the ages.[3]

In the spiritual world which gave birth to Christian prayer and worship Scripture was, as Robert Terwilliger used to put it, 'the Book of the Presence': a place, an occasion of encounter between God and humankind. And yet, as Terwilliger lamented some thirty years ago: 'If in Churches which employ liturgy the Word of God is heard at all, it is in spite of, and not because of, the forms.'[4] It reminds us, he went on, of the 'deep and lasting enmity' that can exist between believers in the Word of God and the traditional worship of the Christian church.[5] Admittedly, the occasion of those thoughts was a period when churches were on the brink of major changes in worship patterns and styles. It might be thought, therefore, that formal worship had recovered the potency of the Word of God in its celebrations. But has it? Is the Word of God in the setting of Sunday worship heard and experienced as the Book of the Presence and as the table at which our languishing hearts and souls are really fed? Or has the power of the

Word at the eucharist in fact been dissipated?[6] For many
it has.

But can any eucharist be adequate when people's
experience of the Word of God is so marginal, so
uncompelling? The Anglican divine Herbert Thorndike,
writing in the seventeenth century, thought not; he
described any eucharist where the Word of God is effectively barred from the apprehension of the worshippers
as a 'half-sacrament'.[7] Admittedly, he was thinking of the
Latin mass celebrated in a foreign tongue. But the criti-
cism still stands, I think, and largely because we fail to
celebrate the service of the Word in a way which makes
the most of its potential for prayerful engagement with
God. Such engagement will never be automatic, never be
a question of form alone; but a first and important step
in nurturing that engagement is to recover the way in
which our Christian forebears celebrated the Word of
God.

The Early Pattern

The service of the Word is more than a succession of
Bible readings. As a form of worship it is meant to
embody the way God calls us and seeks a response of
faith and obedience from us. It is to be an expression in
the present of a way of encounter which reaches back
into the experience of God's people in the depths of
Old Testament history. Of that experience as it was
expressed in the giving of the Law at Mt Sinai mention
has already been made.[8] In the spiritual experience of
the Jews that pattern of encounter remained central. So,
for instance, in the worship of the Jewish synagogue at
the time of Jesus and the first Christians the pattern
was expressed in a succession of readings, together with
chants, which reflected the prayer–shape of divine call

and human response. Synagogue worship, centred on readings from Scripture (a task Jesus himself performed [see Luke. 16.14–21]), began with readings from the Torah, or Law of Moses; then that was followed by a reading from the Prophets whose insights added to the spiritual meaning of what had already been heard. Last of all came the teaching of the community's rabbi who drew out the present significance of what had been heard.[9]

Because so many of the early Christians were Jews they naturally employed that pattern. In addition, they introduced the apostles' commentary (chiefly the New Testament 'Letters' or 'Epistles') in place of the rabbis' teaching. Lastly, they added readings from the Gospels, the words and deeds of Jesus, in the light of which all the other readings found their true meaning. The service of the Word in the Christian eucharist is an adaptation of that Jewish synagogue pattern. From the beginning it sought to embody the two key characteristics of the pattern: first, a Word-centred spirituality rooted in the prayer-shape of call and response; and second, an experience of the readings as a progressive revelation of God's truth and purposes for his people. For many centuries the church in the West read three lessons at each eucharist; then in the Middle Ages it read only two. Other non-western churches even today read more than three. However that may be, the readings taken as a whole have as their aim to offer a call, an immediate invitation to dialogue with God. The overall shape of the service of the Word, therefore, is to address a word to each hearer so that he or she might meet *the* Word in a dialogue of prayer.

That last purpose is clearer still when we look at each reading taken by itself. It has a structure whose various components follow upon one another purposefully and in a kind of ascending movement. The overall goal is this: to foster an encounter with the Word of God.[10]

What is the structure? As we can determine it from early Christian worship the structure was this: after the reading itself came, first, a responsive chant; second, silent prayer offered by each worshipper; and third, a collect offered by the president of the gathering.[11] At the heart of that pattern is an act of proclamation, followed by a response which was both silent and vocal, personal and corporate.

A Living Word

The potential for encounter begins very simply with the proclamation of a scriptural passage. How decisive for the possibility of responsive prayer and praise is that utterance! Sadly, the evocative power of the Word of God has been lessened by several factors which encourage us to play down the experience of the spoken word. For instance, the mass production of Bibles has led us to regard Scripture as something we possess, something we handle and control, and given for an individual's private reading and interpretation. Sometimes people read the Scriptures even as they are being read. The consequence is to lose the experience of the Word as something *heard*. In addition, our easy access to Scripture means that we are in no sense dependent on hearing the Word of God at the eucharist; its connection with the community's praise is lost, so too is its context of prayer. On both counts the experience of the Word of God in worship as our Christian forebears knew it is lessened.

Yet the character and structure of the service of the Word derive from an acute sense of the preciousness of words. Even the written word was engaged in a way that gave scope to its aural richness and evocative power,

since, when the ancients read, they always read aloud,
shaping the words with their mouths and speaking them
even if only in a whisper. As a result their reading was
slower; words, phrases, sentences were approached not
merely as communications to be comprehended intel-
lectually but as things to be encountered by the senses,
to be savoured even, at a unique moment of aural
encounter.

All of this applies to the public reading of Scripture in
worship. Romano Guardini's words are worth quoting in
this regard:

> Solemn reading requires solemn listening, not simul-
> taneous reading. Otherwise, why read aloud at all?
> Our bookish upbringing is to blame for this unnatu-
> ralness. Most deplorably, it encourages people to read
> when they should listen. As a result, the fairy tale has
> died and poetry has lost its power; for its resonant,
> wise, fervent and festive language is meant to be
> heard.[12]

He goes on to say that the word read silently on a page
'remains unfinished, entangled in print, incorporeal;
vital parts are still lacking'. 'No longer', he laments,
'does the sacred word unfold in its full spiritual-corporal
reality and soar through space to the listener, to be
heard and received into his life.'[13] It is not, of course,
true that only through so rich an experience of words
can the Word of God engage us in prayerful dialogue.
But the likelihood of such a dialogue springing from the
proclamation of the Word at the eucharist depends on
reading that is true to the power of the words. The act of
public reading is therefore the critical first element in
the proclamation of the Word. It is designed not chiefly
to instruct or to inform but to allure us into response to
God's loving–kindness in prayer and praise.

But this hearing is meant to be the hearing of the

heart. It is to be received into the depths of our being. The process of deep hearing begins as we actually hear the words spoken. That hearing, however, is but the beginning of a hearing which must reach deeply within us. If those words are to engage us at our spiritual centre something more is needed.

Look well, O soul, upon thyself
lest spiritual ambition
should mislead and blind thee
to thy essential task:
to wait in quietness,
to knock and persevere in humble faith.

Anonymous

It is manifest that our Lord being risen again, and giving the Holy Spirit unto His disciples by breathing on them gave them also a spiritual grace of understanding the Scriptures, as you find where first the disciples that went to Emmaus confess with admiration, 'Did not our hearts burn within us when He talked with us on the way and opened to us the Scriptures?'

Herbert Thorndike

O Lord our God, illumine our minds so that we may pay attention to and understand the sweet voice of your life-giving and divine commandments. Grant us in your grace and mercy that we may gather from your commandments the fruits of love and hope and salvation which are beneficial to the soul and the body, and that we may sing constant praise to you, without ceasing, at all times, Lord of all, Father, Son and Holy Spirit.

The Syro–Malabar Liturgy

5

'Ephphatha! *Be Open!*': *Appropriation*

Of the many possibilities which the eucharist holds open for us one of the greatest is that of conversation with the living Word of God. One of the mysterious qualities of the Word is its power to speak universally, to all, and at the same time personally, to each. We readily admit the authority of the Word of God as a principle of Christian belief. But actually to discern its particular claim upon us is more difficult. And yet every word is a personal communication. 'The word', it has been said,

> is the revelation of a person to a person, of an 'I' to a 'you.' It is the first act whereby someone enters into the life of another someone. Consequently, it is the Word of God which is the revelation of God to us, His personal revelation. And it is by this same Word that God intends to enter into our life.[1]

The service of the Word assumes its proper role when we experience the proclamation of the Word as a personal address to every person who listens. Our belief in the authority of the Word of God should include an awareness of its power to address each of us, to invite us into dialogue.

The Jewish philosopher Martin Buber records a rabbinic vignette which speaks to this point.

Every evening after prayer, the Baal Shem went to his room. Two candles were set in front of him and the mysterious Book of Creation put on the table among other books. Then all those who needed his counsel were admitted in a body, and he spoke to them until the eleventh hour. One evening, when the people left, one of them said to the man beside him how much good the words the Baal Shem had directed to him, had done him. But the other told him not to talk such nonsense, that they had entered the room together and from that moment on the master had spoken to no one except himself. A third, who heard this, joined in the conversation with a smile, saying how curious that both were mistaken, for the rabbi had carried on an intimate conversation with him the entire evening. Then a fourth and a fifth made the same claim, and finally all began to talk at once and tell what they had experienced. But the next instant they all fell silent.[2]

The story is called, appropriately, 'The Address'. The proclamation of the Word at the eucharist is meant to make possible for each of us just such an experience: the Word addressed to *all* and addressed to *each*. Indeed, one of the things meant by Scripture's 'inspiration' is its continuing power to foster an encounter between God and humankind. God is committed to its words as a Presence; he addresses himself to us through them 'as if they were at this instant pronounced for the first time'.[3]

Yet real communication is not a monologue but a dialogue. The divine call, directed to each of us, seeks our response. As Gerard Hughes puts it, God is a 'beckoning' word.[4] Through his Word proclaimed God beckons us toward a meeting, into a conversation. His Word is not to be lodged in the head as a bit of holy information but to descend to the heart, that deepest centre of ourselves. It is an approach to each of us in our absolute uniqueness. The contemporary Egyptian spiritual father Matta el Meskeen puts it this way when he speaks of our encounter with God through Scripture: 'God speaks, and every man on the face of the earth can hear His voice, understand and respond, as if he is being called personally by name.'[5]

Such an understanding of the proclamation of the Word and our response is akin to the ancient Christian practice of 'divine reading', or *lectio divina,* the foundation of all Christian prayer. In fact the early patterns of Christian worship such as the service of the Word at the eucharist give exemplary expression to this 'divine' or 'spiritual reading'. What are its characteristics? First, such reading flowed from a view of Scripture which went beyond the critical and unimaginative ways in which we often approach it. It saw an allegorical or, as it is sometimes called, a contemplative meaning in addition to the literal one.[6] It always involved consideration of Scripture's literal sense but it then went on in search of its further allegorical meaning. An allegorical meaning could be many things; at heart, however, it involved a *personalized* meaning for the individual hearer. The allegorical meaning explores (rather than explains) the scriptural passage as an invitation to dialogue with God in the here and now.

'Speak a Word, Father'

Searching for a 'word' lies at the heart of the spirituality of the early Christians. It is, for instance, a key theme in the spiritual world of the desert fathers, the spiritual masters of the early Christian centuries in Egypt and Palestine. The phrase, despite its links with those first Christian ascetics, points to the 'word'–centred spirituality which all Christians practised.[7] The 'word' which was sought was not a theological explanation, nor a form of pastoral counselling in any modern sense, nor an invitation to analysis or argument. What then was it? To illustrate the character of this 'word' Benedicta Ward recounts how a monk once came to the great St Basil, bishop of Caesarea. 'Speak a word, Father,' he asked. Basil replied: 'Thou shalt love the Lord thy God with all thy heart.' The inquiring monk then went away. Twenty years later the monk returned and said 'Father, I have struggled to keep your word; now speak another word to me.' Basil responded: 'Thou shalt love thy neighbour as thyself.' And the monk returned obediently to his cell to try to keep that word.[8]

Several features of that episode are worth noting. First, the 'word' that is sought is a scriptural phrase or sentence. As in the case of Jesus himself when he replied to questions or challenges, so in the subsequent tradition of Christian prayer the 'word' given is from *the* Word. Second, the response involves deference and obedience. The disciple asks for a 'word' and then receives it. It does not matter whether he likes or approves of the 'word'; he obediently receives it as authoritative in his life. Third, the disciple takes the 'word' away with him. The story implies that he prayed, meditated on, and tried to live the text for twenty years! He lived with the 'word' and the 'word' lived with him. The point surely is that the 'word' was understood through slow and steady rumination, that relentless process of slow digestion like that of a cow chewing the cud.

Such an approach to the Word is typical of all 'divine reading', even that connected with the eucharist. It presumes that Scripture has a life message for each and every hearer, that it reveals a spiritual way which can be followed. That points up another aspect of this 'word'–centred spirituality: the 'word' masters the hearer; the hearer does not master it. Susan Muto puts it this way:

The text [of Scripture] reveals a spiritual way or word
I can follow. As a living mode of communication, it
becomes master to me as disciple. I want the power of
the word to penetrate my life. A shift has taken place
from myself as master of the word to myself as servant
of the word. It is now I who am the disciple; the text
is master. The truth contained in the text is the standard against which I am judged. It is not I who judge
the text but the text that judges me.[9]

What is at stake in such a relationship to the text is the
possibility of either 'encountering' or 'countering' the
text.[10] In the latter case we exercise mastery through
reactions based on our accustomed or preferred stan-
dards of judgement ('too old', 'archaic', 'sexist', 'dogmatic', etc.). But in the former case the text is received
as an invitation to discipleship. It is the basis of a spiritual dialogue which guides one's life.[11]

In the service of the Word where 'divine reading' is
also 'divine hearing' the same principles apply. Whether
it involves just one of the lessons read, or a portion of it,
or the accumulated message of the whole series is unim-
portant so long as a 'word' is heard, the beckoning of
Jesus Christ *the* Word who ceaselessly knocks at the door
of our hearts.

Be Still and Know

The possibilities surrounding this act of hearing find
their source in the silence which follows each Scripture
reading. Indeed, our contemporary service books are
notable for their explicit instruction or recommendation
that after a given Scripture reading 'silence may be
kept'.[12] It is, in fact, one of the most radical reforms to
our celebration of the eucharist that it can now integrate
silence in a positive way. Its significance lies precisely in

relation to the task of appropriation which is our chief response to the act of proclamation.

In the case of silence in collective praying I spoke of its active quality: the silence allows space for the active offering of personal petitionary prayer.[13] In the service of the Word the silence is of a different kind. First and foremost it is a passive silence. Its primary aim is to enable us to attend to, to 'hear and receive' (to use Cranmer's phrase) God's holy Word. In the Byzantine liturgy before each reading the deacon cries to the worshippers 'Let us attend!' to remind them that the readings are not just to be heard but to be engaged with attentively. That is what this silence is for: our attentive engagement with the 'word' within the words. It is a time for *God* the Word to speak. How do we 'hear and receive' that 'word'? First, amid the richness of the words with their wealth of themes, images, commands and insights the attentive heart may be struck by one particular word (e.g. 'glory', 'light', 'love', 'darkness', 'repent'). Or it may be a phrase as in the case of the 'word' which St Basil gave to the monk who besought him: 'Thou shalt love the Lord thy God with all thy heart'; or another such as 'The word was made flesh and dwelt among us'; or 'It is not I who lives but Christ within me', or just 'Christ within me'. It is best if they are committed to memory.[14] It could be a visual image in the mind which a word or episode suggests: the crucified Lord; the descent of the Spirit; a scene of healing. In both cases out of the words a 'word' may come, and through that 'word' *the* Word may be trying to engage us.

This is not a process which can be neatly timed or contained. The silent space afforded within the service is a kind of springboard, the beginning of a potentially endless meditation on the meaning of a given text. But the 'word' will be recognized as such because it somehow begins, even then, to take root within us, to call for a response from our depths. 'Thy words do finde me out,' the Anglican priest-poet George Herbert once wrote in his poem 'The Holy Scriptures (II)'. The 'word' will carry an inspirational power for the hearer's life.[15] It might begin with our imaginations, setting ourselves, our present life, within the text, that is, within the circumstances and personalities which it presents. The 'word' of Scripture becomes part of *our* journey now.[16] 'Read of what has been done as though it were happening now,' was Ludolph of Saxony's advice on reading the Gospels.[17] His maxim applies to all 'divine reading'. Indeed one of the reasons for the succession of readings at the eucharist going back through the Old Testament to the primeval history of humankind – stories which sometimes seem far removed from us in their archaic character – is because through baptism the whole history of God's people becomes our history. In a spiritual sense that history is relived in each one of us.[18]

Thus through the silence which is kept after each reading, proclamation leads on to appropriation. The effectiveness of the silence will, of course, vary from person to person and from time to time. Coming to terms with such silence in a spiritually fruitful way ought to be a principal aim of any spiritual discipline. Most of us find the art of stillness and silence elusive and hard. But there is no doubt that the integrity of our prayer at the eucharist depends upon each member of the congregation learning the discipline of hearing and receiving the 'word' through the words.

In the case of the Old and New Testament readings the pattern of proclamation through public reading and the response of appropriation through silent prayer is clear. But what of the Gospel reading? As the climax of the succession of readings the Gospel presents the fulfilment of God's saving purposes in Christ. Yet that fulfilment is not merely in the past; it is an ever present and ever powerful Spirit-borne message. Hence, the Gospel proclamation too seeks to engage men and women in each successive age and in every new moment. As Christ the Word of God took flesh in the womb of the Mother of God so that same Word of Good News seeks a home in the womb of our lives. 'God wishes always and everywhere to work the mystery of his Incarnation,' St Maximus the Confessor once commented.[19] The mystery of Christ our head is to become the mystery of us his body. And so, in hearing the Gospel too our response is to personalize the message, to hear the Word through the words, to meet the Word through his 'word'.

Whereas that meeting is fostered by silent meditation after the Old and New Testament readings, after the Gospel it is fostered by the spoken meditation or sermon. Thus the sermon, which is rightly seen as part of the 'rhythmic ritual' of the eucharist,[20] takes its place within the movement from proclamation to appropriation. Often the act of preaching is described as the proclamation of the Gospel, but strictly speaking it is part of the act of appropriation since its aim is not simply to articulate the Good News but to root it in the lives of its contemporary hearers, to transform the past action of God into a 'contemporaneous dynamic reality'.[21] Preaching is the process of 'actuating' Scripture (to use John Donne's word) so that they might become '*our* scriptures'.[22]

So, the place of the sermon is squarely within the responsive act of appropriation which follows every act of proclamation. Its sacramental power – remember that our early Christian forebears did not distinguish the service of the Word from the 'sacramental' part of the service[23] – lies precisely in its success in bringing the personal Word of God present in Scripture into the lives of those assembled to hear, receive and celebrate it.

Speech is the organ of the present world. Silence is the mystery of the world to come.

St Isaac the Syrian

Out of Christ all that is behind is dead. We cannot legitimately knit together moment to moment or limb to limb. But in Him the whole dead past becomes alive again: it is part of His body and His life flows through every part.

F. J. A. Hort

Liturgical silence is purposeful, pregnant and controlled – the thunderous quiet of people communicating that which escapes being put into words.

Aidan Kavanaugh

Our silence is a joyful and God-centred silence. It demands of us constant self-denial and plunges us into the deep silence of God where aloneness with God becomes a reality.

Mother Teresa

6

'He Who Sings
Prays Twice': Exultation

'Faith cannot be silent,' Martin Luther once wrote, 'but must say and teach what it knows about God, to the glory of God and the instruction of man.'[1] His comment, part of an extended remark on the nature of singing inspired by Psalm 118, is a most succinct explanation for the words of St Augustine used in the title of this chapter. There is a power in our meeting with God's Word such that its appropriation is deeply bound up with exultation. Response to God's Word is doxological, that is, it naturally involves the glorification of God. The God of the Scriptures, the one who acts to save his people and establishes with them a covenant of love, is a God worthy of praise and worship. With that awareness we are led to consider the third element in the reading and hearing of the Word: exultation.

The Bible itself witnesses to the correspondence between proclamation and exultation. The acts of God which it describes are often highlighted by hymns and songs. The story of Jesus' birth and infancy as told by St Luke is a vivid example. So too are St Paul's letters. His presentation of the Good News to his hearers is frequently complemented by the use of hymns adapted from early Christian worship, and in a less formal way his occasional outbursts of praise to God for what he has done in Christ have a hymnic quality. Similarly, the

Book of Revelation is marked by recurring choruses of
praise as the final and victorious purposes of God are
envisioned.[2]

Such a combination of proclamation and exultation
signals the Jewish ethos of the first Christians' experience. It was a long-standing awareness on the part of the
Jews that the wonderful deeds of God were a cause of
deep joy and, therefore, of exultation in song. Indeed,
their joy in the Word of God was such that within the
sphere of worship Scripture itself was sung rather than
said, as was the people's response in the form of chants
and hymns.

Song as Response

Therein lies the rationale for the third ingredient in the
experience of 'divine reading' within the service of the
Word: the psalm, canticle or hymn. Our meeting with
the Word of God is always a cause of joy, so that proclamation and appropriation give rise to exultation. The
response of exultant song, deeply rooted in the Jewish
experience of the Word of God, was given a permanent
place in Christian worship very early. In keeping with
those roots, therefore, the Christians' eucharist sought
to maintain the close link between proclamation, appropriation and exultation. The order of the three components may have varied (e.g., silence may have followed
singing, sometimes the other way around). Most importantly, though, each element was viewed as an integral
part of encounter with the Word of God at the eucharist.

The early Christian pattern in which responsive song
was integral made much of the Psalms. They formed the
core of the Christian hymnal so that each reading from
Scripture was followed by a chanted psalm.[3] The pattern
could repeat itself again and again, just as it does still in
the vigil service of readings on Easter Eve.[4] Within the

eucharist itself the number of readings gradually shrank; then the sung responses were shortened and eventually extracted from the sphere of congregational participation. The experience of each reading of the Word was thus fundamentally distorted. In the long run it gave rise to 'a great and unwholesome silence', namely, the demise of any element of song as a natural and regular part of worshippers' response to God's Word.[5]

In the spirituality and worship of the Reformation music and song returned as part of the rediscovery of the Word of God. Luther's complaint against the 'bleating and bellowing of cathedrals and monasteries' was not an indictment of liturgical singing in itself. In fact, Luther viewed Christian song as the fitting expression of the deep, unconquerable joy of faith – faith as confidence in the saving purposes of God in the face of anything and everything.[6] That sense of jubilation in response to God's Word gave rise to the Reformation hymn tradition. Its basic rationale was the same as the psalmody of ancient Christian worship: 'the exultation of our whole being, nourished in the contemplation of the Mystery discovered in the Word'.[7]

In the eucharistic worship of the English *Book of Common Prayer* the rationale which connected proclamation with exultation was lost sight of but the devotional value of song in worship was vigorously maintained. In his *Laws of Ecclesiastical Polity* Richard Hooker invoked the testimony of St Basil in support of the 'edifying' value of psalm singing. In the seventeenth century Herbert Thorndike, inspired by early Christian patterns, espoused 'the interweaving of the lessons with hymns' precisely because it served 'to preserve attention and quicken devotion'.[8] Here we are closer, by intention at least, to an integrated view of proclamation and exultation such as was described above.

For Perfecting Holiness

But why this integration of word, silence and song? As has already been suggested, there is the aspect of joy. There is joy in the knowledge of what God, in his great love, has done for us in Jesus Christ. Yet there is more. There is, for instance, the power of music to integrate aspects of experience and awareness which are easily separated. In the act of singing, intellect, emotions, imagination, will, and even body are joined in a common and simultaneous effort. It is suggested as well by one writer that the experience of song in worship can actually extend our powers of understanding. 'Action and knowledge', he writes, 'are always linked with the enthusiasm which in worship gives birth to song. This hymn of worship expands the active and cognitive powers of the soul, widens the horizons of what is known and can be known.'[9] His remark is akin to that of another theologian who, writing out of the exuberant singing tradition of Methodism, describes music and song as a place where fuller sensibilities, often stifled in the cut and thrust of everyday life, can be rediscovered. Little wonder, then, that Luther saw in song a power that went beyond purely rational 'comprehending'.

It has also been said that song has an enabling force. It empowers new resolutions of the will, new commitments. As a result it heightens the overall disposition of obedience and faithfulness in those who sing.[10] That was the power of song in the life of the soul which John Wesley so prized: it worked 'for perfecting holiness in the fear of God'.[11]

What is striking in this threefold description of the effect of song in worship is its similarity to those things we expect from prayer: integrating disparate aspects of our being, extending our powers of understanding beyond the merely rational or analytical, and enabling a greater commitment of will through deeper obedience to God. St Augustine was right to describe Christian song as doubly intense prayer! Is it too much, then, to suppose that an appreciation of this congruity between prayer and song has guided the place of song in the worship of the eucharist? There is, I think, a basic connection, even complementarity, between the prayerful appropriation of the Word and the corporate exultation of believers expressing themselves in songs of praise.

Such insights may compel us to reconsider the actual pattern of each Scripture reading at the eucharist in terms of liturgical logic. The form of this responsive act of exultation will vary as it has in the history of Christian worship throughout the ages. In the Catholic Church Gregorian chant acquired pre-eminence as *the* music of the liturgy whereas in the Reformed Churches metrical psalmody and chorales took its place. The Anglican tradition developed its own tradition of chants and anthem repertoire, and became increasingly eclectic in adapting the best of virtually every Christian musical tradition. The Wesleys' collection of hymns, that 'little body of experimental and practical divinity',[12] was a tremendous enrichment of the tradition of sung prayer and praise. In the end, though, the musical genre is far less important than understanding the place of Christian song in relation to the prayer–shape of the eucharist and, particularly, as an integral part of worshippers' response to the proclamation of the Word. It is worth noting the continuing power and attraction of the services of lessons and carols common in Advent and at Christmas. There each reading from Scripture is complemented by music in diverse styles, and all combine into a sublime pattern of extended meditation on God's gracious acts recorded in the pages of the Bible. We often fail to realize that the essential structure of those services is very much like what has been described above, where hearing and receiving the Word of God gives rise to song, 'words in which faith does not reason, does not even describe, but sings what it believes'.[13]

The Poetry of Belief

How does the Nicene Creed fit within this pattern of proclamation, prayer and praise? As a feature of the eucharist it was introduced in the sixth century and slowly acquired a regular and universally recognized place. It might be thought, therefore, that it has no place within the pattern plotted so far. On the contrary. The creed finds its natural place, I think, within the framework of this responsive exultation in song which accompanies the proclamation of the Word. That may seem strange in light of how we often experience the creed: a long, concentrated theological statement in seemingly archaic prose. Indeed it is sometimes argued that for that very reason the creed should be used far less or dropped altogether from eucharistic worship except on major occasions.

I disagree. It is important to realize that even the elaborate Nicene Creed grew out of a long tradition of faith affirmation whose origins lie in believers' responses in the service of baptism.[14] 'Do you believe in God the Father?' 'I believe in God the Father Almighty . . . ' 'Do you believe in Jesus Christ, the Son of God?' 'I believe in Jesus Christ, his only Son, our Lord.' 'Do you believe in God the Holy Spirit?' 'I believe in the Holy Spirit . . . '[15] Early on such responses were assembled into a declaration which we know as the Apostles' Creed. The longer Nicene Creed, used at the eucharist, is but an expansion of the key affirmations of the Apostles' Creed. The point is that the creed is, in its basic inspiration and intent, a *response* to God's saving acts in his Word Jesus Christ.

What sort of response is the creed? We commonly view it as an authoritative doctrinal statement of key Christian truths, a kind of 'agreed statement' among the churches of the early centuries. To a great extent that is true, and the first impulse to add the creed to the eucharist was in fact so that it might serve as a guide to correct belief. But that is just the starting point in a consideration of what creeds are and how they are understood and used liturgically.

It is interesting that early writers who explained the meaning of the eucharist, without denying the use of the creed as a rule of right faith, viewed the creed with an emphasis on its character as a hymn of praise to God. Dionysius the Areopagite, who wrote a commentary on the eucharist in the sixth century, described it as 'the universal song of praise' and 'the catholic hymn'.[16] He wished to emphasize its hymnic, praise character. Dionysius went on to note how some people refer to the credal 'hymn' as a 'confession of praise' or as a 'symbol [i.e. collection] of adoration' and a 'hierarchic thanksgiving'. 'To me,' Dionysius acknowledged, 'it seems that this song is a celebration of all the works of God on our behalf.' In viewing the creed as 'containing in it all the spiritual gifts which flow from heaven upon us, the whole mystery of our salvation', Dionysius saw the creed as a concentrated statement of the marvellous saving acts of God fulfilled in Jesus Christ and the Holy Spirit. The creed is in continuity with the psalms which recount the saving deeds of God (e.g. Psalms 105, 106 and 107). Two centuries after Dionysius St Maximus the Confessor described the creed similarly as 'the thanksgiving for the manner of our salvation'.[17]

Not surprisingly these writers think of the creed as a hymn, like the psalms of salvation which their descriptions recall. That meant that the singing of the hymn was the most appropriate way to experience it. All the more so since the saving works of God which it recounts are the basis of what Maximus called 'the divine delight and enjoyment' which God's loving kindness, revealed in the Good News, prompts in those who respond in faith.[18] In keeping with that earlier Christian sense of the hymnic character of the creed one modern writer encourages us to view the creed as a 'sacred poem' or a 'confessional litany' since, he says, in its subtlety of language and careful craftedness the creed makes faith and theology poetic. He goes on to say that when viewed as a sonnet of faith the creed can become 'the protestation of a personal love'.[19] The Anglican Prayer Book tradition nurtured something of this sensibility through the Elizabethan composer John Merbecke's masterly chant setting of the Communion service which included the Nicene Creed. It may well have been with that experience in mind that in the seventeenth century Anthony Sparrow recalled Dionysius' description of the creed as 'the catholic hymn of praise'.

But the custom of singing this 'catholic hymn' has all but died. As a consequence so has our sense of the poetic, hymnic character of the creed. It may be, however, that a rediscovery of the element of exultation in response to the proclamation of the Word will help us reclaim the creed's character as a hymn of praise. The creed is best seen, then, in relation to the threefold pattern of proclamation, appropriation and exultation surrounding every Scripture reading at the eucharist. The Gospel reading is followed by the sermon, a spoken meditation by which the Word is personalized; that homiletic space for appropriation is in turn followed by the hymnic response of exultation in the form of the sung creed. How appropriate that is. As the credal song ends the patterned sequence of the proclamation of the Word, so that creed gives concise voice to our faithful and joyful testimony to what God has done 'for us and for our salvation'.

Let the word of Christ dwell in you richly . . . and sing psalms and hymns and spiritual songs with thankfulness in your hearts to God.

The Letter to the Colossians (RSV)

The musical experience . . . is also a kind of knowledge, and the knowledge it conveys comes to one with the assurance of conviction.

C. E. M. Joad

The eternal exultation of our future life will be the praise of God, and no one can be fitted for that future life who has not exercised himself in praise in this present life.

St Augustine of Hippo

Praise should be the perpetual pulsation of the soul.

G. K. Chesterton

The words and thoughts of the Psalms spring not only from the unsearchable depths of God, but also from the inmost heart of the Church, and there are no songs which better express her soul, her desires, her longing, her sorrows and her joys.

Thomas Merton

A creed is something to live by, not simply to learn by rote. A creed is also a summary of faith. Each clause is a highly concentrated and highly charged 'nucleus' of Christian thought and belief and experience. At one moment it means little or nothing, and at another moment it can mean everything. Each of us needs the rest of the Church to back up our individual saying of the Creed. When we are weak, others may be strong and vice versa.

Eric Abbott

7

For the Life of the World:
Intercession

'Intercession', it has been said, 'is one of the supreme and costly privileges of the Christian.'[1] It has been so from the beginning of the Christian movement. There can be no surprise, therefore, to discover that when the Christians' eucharist began to take formal shape intercessory prayer had a place in it. An early Christian writer named Justin, describing the eucharist as it was celebrated about the year AD 150, put it like this:

> On the day named after the sun, all who live in city or countryside assemble, and the memoirs of the apostles or the writings of the prophets are read for as long as time allows. When the lector has finished, the president addresses us, admonishing us and exhorting us to imitate the splendid things we have heard. *Then we all stand and pray . . .* [2]

That description testifies to the seriousness with which our Christian forebears saw their task as intercessors when they gathered to celebrate the eucharist.

It was the beginning of a rich tradition of intercessory prayer at the eucharist which in recent years churches have tried to recover. This 'long neglected ingredient'[3] of our worship has taken on new, more participatory forms, and its scope has been enlarged to embrace current and global issues. For all that, however, the prayers of

intercession at the eucharist are so often experienced as
the least adequate, prayerful or purposeful part of a
community's eucharistic celebration.

Part of the problem is surely the practical way in
which the intercessory prayers are planned and executed.
But there is, I believe, a deeper problem still: namely,
our failure to see how intercessory prayer relates to the
eucharist as a whole. The purpose of this chapter, therefore, is to sketch the place of intercession within the
prayer-shape of the eucharist. In light of that prayer-
shape intercession finds its rationale within the overall
structure of the eucharist; and that in turn may help us
to see and use our act of intercession more fruitfully.

With the prayers of intercession the second act in
the eucharistic journey begins. The Godward call to
humankind expressed in the proclamation of the Word
gives rise to our manward response. The first expression
of our response is to pray for others. We have, it is true,
already noted the presence of responsive elements in the
act of proclamation itself. Now that responsive aspect
comes to the fore.

What is intercession? When he described Christian
prayer Michael Ramsey did so in refreshingly simple
terms. Petition, he used to say, is being before God
asking for ourselves; adoration is being before God won-
dering; meditation is being before God considering; and
penitence is being before God with regret for wrongs
committed. Similarly, intercession is being before God
asking on behalf of others.[4] We should add to Ramsey's
description this equally simple realization: those different kinds of prayer – intercession, penitence, and thanksgiving, for instance – are all *responses* to God's truth and
presence. That is the overlooked significance of the posi-
tion of the prayers of intercession *after* the proclamation
of the Word. The prayer-shape of proclamation and
response highlights the responsive character of all

intercession. But why is intercession part of our *responsive* prayer to God?

The Kingdom Context

The responsive quality of intercessory prayer is best grasped by asking the question: why intercede? In some religions intercession has little place in the life of prayer. Some religions, for instance, are fatalistic in outlook: the human situation, whatever it may be for individuals or for whole societies, is given and cannot be changed by human action or intercession. It must be accepted for what it is. The Christian view is different. Christians see the world, and each and every human circumstance, as the arena of God's activity for transfiguration and salvation. The Old Testament is an account of God's activity first in creating the world; and then, in its fallen condition, in calling a holy people, Israel, to himself. In Jesus Christ and through the ongoing work of the Holy Spirit we believe that God's loving purposes will be brought to fulfilment. The Bible, as God's Word to and for us, is the fascinating, dynamic, tragic, joyful record of God's undying determination to complete his promises. We have already seen how the progressive shape of the liturgy of the Word seeks, first, to show God's transforming presence in human history; and then, how it seeks to connect our individual and communal histories to that same presence and power. When understood this way the liturgy of the Word encourages us to hope and to pray for comparable marvellous, transforming deeds here and now, in our lives and in the lives of others. Through the Good News proclaimed by Jesus we live in the hope that all circumstances and people can be touched and changed by the redemptive work of Christ and the transforming work of the Spirit. To intercede, therefore, is to live in the confidence that, in the words of an eloquent ancient collect, things which were cast down might be raised up, and things which had grown old might be made new, and that all things might be brought to their perfection in Christ.[5]

But how are we to pray thus? Here too the character of intercession as a form of responsive prayer is important. So often, it seems, intercessory prayer appears as an accumulation of arbitrary requests to God. Often they seem to be the expression of personal whim, an assertion of 'the world as I think it ought to be'. The urge to turn intercession into something like that is psychologically understandable but spiritually and liturgically misguided. Christian intercession is offered in the trust and hope in *God's* transforming purposes.

No less importantly, that trust is given shape and direction by God's work and will revealed in creation, and then in his works 'for us and for our salvation' culminating in the coming of Jesus Christ and the sending of the Spirit. That is the story of God's acts and words which Scripture, read in the first part of the eucharist, expresses. So, as one modern writer has put it, intercession does not spring primarily from a sense of our own or others' needs but from an attentive listening to the Word of God where all our deepest human needs are declared.[6] Our intercession is cast in the framework of those words of the Lord's Prayer: 'thy will be done on earth as it is in heaven'. Intercessory prayer is part of our prayerful response to God's Word because our prayer is meant to bridge the needs of others and of the world, on the one hand, and the Gospel vision of God's kingdom, on the other. Whereas many generous and concerned people see and seek to meet human needs, Christians are called to place those needs in their kingdom context, and that we do through authentic response to the Word of God. Indeed, only in that kingdom context – the standpoint of a distinct perspective on the world – will some things be discerned as needs at all. In the end, therefore, intercessory prayer means seeing the world in Christ, as it really is or ought to be, above and beyond our partial points of view, our limited and limiting agendas.[7]

What has been said so far highlights both the similarities and the differences between petition and intercession. Once again, Evelyn Underhill's remark about the clear categorization of prayer in our western tradition of worship ought to be kept in mind. We should, for instance, distinguish petitionary prayer, that is, prayer for ourselves individually and as a local community gathered for prayer, from intercessory prayer which focuses on the wider, even universal needs of the church and of the world, as well as on those who are absent from the immediate worshipping congregation. When collective prayer is petitionary in the way described in chapter three then the intercessory prayers of the eucharist can become a period of self-forgetful prayer on behalf of others.

One of the benefits of the old fixed forms of intercession such as that found in earlier editions of the *Book of Common Prayer* was that it disallowed any lapses into prayer for ourselves – petitionary prayer, strictly speaking. At the same time, as was the case with the collect, that older style tended to be impersonal. It did not allow any place for intercessory prayer to be offered by worshippers themselves. In neither structure nor execution did it seek to unite personal and corporate intercession.

It was not always so. As in the case of the collects, so here early Christian worship sought to co-ordinate the prayer of the whole body gathered to pray – the corporate prayer – with prayers offered by its individual members. In fact, early forms of intercession actually took the form of collective prayer as it was described in an earlier chapter. That is, each intercession was introduced by a 'bidding', or invitation to prayer, in which the object of intercession was stated (e.g. the church, the civil authorities, the sick). Then a space for silent prayer followed, when each person offered his or her intercessions concerning the matter bidden. Finally, those individual prayers were gathered in a collect prayer offered by the head of the worshipping group.[8] Other litany forms of intercession developed which tried in different ways to integrate the prayers of individuals with the prayer of the congregation as a whole.

Christ's Intercession and Ours

The shape of intercessory prayer, like that of collective prayer, points to the basis of our privilege and power to intercede. Just as clearly as in collective prayer, in intercession too the joining of the personal prayer of those gathered to the formal prayer offered by the head of the assembly expresses the mystical reality of the church, 'the whole Christ': Christ at the head of his body, the people of God, who offer their prayer *through* him. Once again, the body language of the community gathered at the eucharist is an image of those who live *in* Christ by baptism: God's people gathered around Christ their head, present with their brother and Lord offering prayer to God through him.

In considering this act of intercession we are drawn unavoidably to that truth in the high-priestly intercession of Christ described in the Letter to the Hebrews. As the perfection of all priesthood, the writer affirms, Christ is the eternal intercessor of his people: 'he is able for all time to save those who approach God through him, since he always lives to make intercession for them' (7.25 NRSV). The passage indicates our acceptance by God in our various and continuing needs. But it would be odd to stop there. For if Christ is an intercessor before God with us, his people, gathered around him and sharing his life, then the intercessory character of his life should in some way become an essential quality of our life in him.[9]

The intercession of Christ himself as well as our intercession *in* him finds its motivation in love and the solidarity with others which love engenders. 'It is the very nature of love', it has been said with regard to intercession, 'to give up and forget itself for the sake of others. It takes their needs and makes them its own.'[10] Those words are echoed in the remarks of a modern Orthodox theologian who, writing on the intercessory prayer of the eucharist, reminds us that 'to be in Christ means to be like Him, to make ours the very movement of His life. And as He "ever liveth to make intercession" for all "that come unto God by Him" (Heb. 7.25) so we cannot help accepting His intercession as our own.'[11] In a similar vein Michael Ramsey captured the foundation and motive of our intercessory prayer at the eucharist when he remarked that there in a supreme way 'the people of Christ are, through our great high priest, with God with the world around on their hearts'.[12]

So then, intercessory prayer arises at the eucharist as our first main response to the Gospel vision received in the proclamation of the Word. Equally, as a response made possible in and through Jesus Christ it is patterned on his eternal intercession as he stands before the Father with the needs of his brothers and sisters, indeed of the whole world, close to him.

I have reason to count this service the most eminent service that Christians can offer to God, and those prayers the most effectual that they address unto him.

Herbert Thorndike

If 'the Father knoweth', why should we ask for anything, as we do in the Lord's Prayer and other prayers? What matters in such prayers is our act of turning consciously to God, our humility, the feeling of connection and dependence; and besides this, there is the importance of framing things explicitly in words, of communion.

Alexander Elchaninov

We cannot possibly speak of prayer in terms of man-made rules. Somehow we have to enter into the heart and mind and will of the Praying Christ Himself. Our discipline of prayer includes such a close fellowship of our Lord in His desires that we become interceders. Where love is, there intercession is.

Eric Abbott

A Christian fellowship lives and exists by the intercession of its members for one another, or it collapses.

Dietrich Bonhoeffer

The liturgical assembly is the world being renovated according to the divine pleasure – not as patient being passively worked upon but as active agent faithfully co-operating in its own rehabilitation. What one witnesses in the liturgy is the world being done as the world's Creator and Redeemer will the world to be done.

Aidan Kavanaugh

The praying Christian . . . draws inspiration from the world for which he prays. Sometimes the beauty he sees in the world will stir him to wonder and to worship. Sometimes the presence of the divine word in human lives of goodness or wisdom will stir him with gratitude and reverence. The presence of self-sacrifice in human lives will set him thinking of Calvary. More often perhaps the agony of the world will draw him to the compassion of Jesus and stir his will to pray. He will know that by their worship and their prayer Christians serve the world powerfully . . . By their praying the Christians are helping the world to recover the soul which the world has lost.

Michael Ramsey

8

The Kingdom of Conversion: Penitence

In his famous *Life* of the Egyptian desert monk Anthony the Great (251?–356) St Athanasius tells the story of Anthony's 'conversion'. His parents died when he was a young man of eighteen or so. About six months later Anthony was going to church and reflected, as he went, on the way the apostles left everything, followed Jesus, and even sold their possessions for distribution to those in need. 'Pondering over these things,' his biographer continued,

> he entered the church, and it happened the Gospel was being read; and he heard the Lord saying to the rich man (Matt. 19.21), 'If thou wouldest be perfect, go and sell that thou hast and give to the poor; and come follow Me and then thou shalt have treasure in heaven.' Anthony, as though God had put him in mind of the saints, and the message had been read on his account, went out immediately from the church, and gave the possessions of his forefathers to the villagers.[1]

That story of St Anthony's conversion to a radical obedience to the Gospel is recognized as a pattern and example for countless other followers of Christ through Christian history. Aspects of his experience reappear in the recorded lives of figures such as the complex St

65

Augustine of Hippo and the simple St Francis of Assisi.[2] Those who find the account of Anthony's conversion so compelling usually do so on account of the radical, decisive and generous quality of his response to the words of Jesus. As such, of course, the account stands as an enduring challenge to all Christians to hear and embrace the hard sayings of the Lord.

But the story of St Anthony's conversion has more to tell us. The setting of Anthony's life-changing encounter with God was at the Christian eucharist. As St Athanasius records it, it came as a response to the proclamation of the Word in a reading from St Matthew's Gospel. I note this because it sheds light on the theme of penitential prayer with which this chapter is concerned. For here, as in the preceding chapter, the task is to highlight the place of the confession of sin, or General Confession, within the prayer–shape of the eucharist, and to see how it contributes toward the gradually deepening encounter with God through the acts of proclamation and response. On both accounts that vivid story about St Anthony's conversion provides important clues.

Penitence and confession of sin both relate to the biblical idea of repentance. But does that story of St Anthony have to do with repentance? At first glance it might not appear to since we usually think of repentance as a feeling of regret leading, perhaps, to an acknowledgement of sins committed. Yet the episode from the *Life of St Anthony* involves no such thing. It is, however, a story of repentance, not according to our popular notion of that word, but according to the sense of the word typical in the New Testament.

The New Testament, especially the teaching of Jesus in the Gospels, speaks little of penitence or the confession of sin *per se*. At the same time, Jesus speaks much of repentance. A 'turning around', a whole change in direction or perspective is what the Greek New Testament word *metanoia*, or 'repentance', means. John the Baptist explicitly called men and women to 'repent' as a necessary preparation for the coming of the Messiah. Jesus, though not declaring the challenge in quite the stark way in which John the Baptist did, called for a deep change of heart and mind and life-style from his hearers. The vividness of the Gospels arises in large measure from the variety of human responses to that challenge to 'repent!'

Repentance as Response

This view of repentance, one which involves the whole person reoriented toward God, must not obscure the equally important recognition that such repentance is an inevitable part of the human response to the Word of God. In the Gospels that Word has the form and moral force of a man named Jesus of Nazareth. He called for repentance from the men and women who met or heard him, and throughout the New Testament, indeed through the subsequent history of the church, that same personal Word still speaks. He still calls each and every hearer to take a radical step, to be re-cast into the new image of Jesus Christ. That episode of St Anthony's conversion with which this chapter opened is but one example of that Word powerfully active through the words of Scripture calling for a response of repentance from those who hear. As for St Anthony, so for everyone repentance is a response to the Word of God. It arises out of an awareness by the hearer that our life is judged by the Word and in need of radical readjustment, even re-creation (2 Cor. 5.17), under its searching light.

That responsive character of penitence has practical consequences for the shape of the eucharist. Many worshippers are now used to an order of service in which the confession of sin comes at the very beginning as an aspect of preparation for the eucharist.[3] But those acquainted with the tradition of the *Book of Common Prayer* will know that ever since Cranmer's first Prayer Book of 1549 the General Confession (as it came to be called) always followed the reading of Scripture at the eucharist. It was a stroke of genius because it gave concrete expression to the Reformers' sense of the convicting, converting power of the Word of God. Although from one point of view he was innovating when he placed the General Confession after the service of the Word, from another point of view he was reintroducing a genuinely biblical experience of confession of sin as conversion in response to the Word proclaimed. Little wonder, therefore, that discussion of penitential prayer should come here. If the traditional Prayer Book pattern is maintained then our consideration of responsive prayer leads naturally from intercession to confession.

It might be argued that the General Confession as typically enacted gives little scope for a real act of repentance. Is it not, people sometimes say, an expression of the general sinfulness of all people and a request for forgiveness on behalf of the world? Is it, in other words, an act of personal penitence or not? In fact, the origins of the act of confession in the eucharist place it squarely in the domain of personal penitence. Certainly commentators on the Anglican Prayer Book were keen to see it in those terms. Charles Wheatley, for instance, in his widely read *Rational Illustration of the Book of Common Prayer* remarked of the General Confession,

> that every single person, who makes this general confession with his lips, may at the same time mentally unfold the plague of his own heart, his particular sins, whatever they may be, as effectually to God, who searches the heart, as if he enumerated them in the most ample form.[4]

'For', he explained, 'a common confession ought to be so

contrived, that every person present may truly speak it as his own case.'[5] So then, although general or, to use Wheatley's word, 'common', the confession at the eucharist is to be an occasion for genuinely personal confession of sin. Surely it is to encourage just that personalization of the penitential act that modern service books often add the direction before the confession is actually said: 'Silence may be kept'.[6]

Can we, however, establish more clearly the link between the proclamation of the Word which forms the first part of the prayer-shape of the eucharist, and the responsive act of penitential prayer in the second? An answer begins with the Exhortation in the *Book of Common Prayer* (1662). There, in setting the stage for the confession of sin, the worshippers are exhorted to examine their lives and conduct 'by the rule of God's commandments' so that 'you may perceive wherein you have offended in what you have done or left undone, whether in thought, word, or deed'. The link between the Word of God – 'God's commandments' – and repentance through penitential prayer is clear. Implicit in it is the notion of penitence as a response to God's Word, and its basic inspiration is the New Testament's idea of repentance: turning one's self Godward, a turning away from specific acts and behaviour which fall short of God's vision for us. The prayer-shape of the eucharist is such that our response to God's Word naturally includes penitential prayer. It is natural because our awareness of what our sin is, of what conversion is needed, only comes to Christians when we see ourselves in the light of the message of the Gospel.

Inverse Perspective

The experience of sight and vision can be used to illustrate this point further. The art of Orthodox

iconography (after the Greek word *eikōn* or 'image')
seeks to present the events of the Bible with the eyes of
faith. They present not photographic exactness but the
kingdom dimension of the event.[7] That striving to con-
vey the kingdom dimension accounts for the seemingly
peculiar features of icons. Perhaps the most bewildering
feature is what is called 'inverse perspective'. Whereas to
natural sight objects become smaller in the distance,
according to the principle of inverse perspective such
objects become larger. This characteristic is a conscious
attempt to communicate visually the awareness that in
the kingdom of God the proportions, the perspectives,
the expectations of the world are changed. 'The last
shall be first and the first shall be last' (Mark 10.31);
'Blessed are the poor' (Matt. 5.3); 'Blessed are those who
mourn' (Matt. 5.4). The one by whom all things were
made is killed on the cross. Out of death comes life. The
Gospel story is a huge tableau of such disturbing inver-
sions of all we ought to expect. Just as that kingdom
perspective provides the context for Christians' intercession, as the previous chapter tried to show, so it is the
measure according to which we are deemed to be saints
and sinners.

In practice, penitential prayer at the eucharist may
provide occasion for the confession of sins which have
been brought from outside, so to speak: sins which have
pricked our consciences as a result of the lifelong ebb
and flow of meditation upon the Bible. But at each celebration of the eucharist there is the opportunity for a
specific encounter with the inverted kingdom perspective of Jesus and the New Testament writers. In light of
that vision of the kingdom, however each person hears
and receives it, he or she is judged. We are judged not by
the skewed values of this world but by the far more
radical 'ethics of the Gospel'.[8] In light of those gospel
ethics, revealed to us in our dialogue with the Word of

God, we can know whether and how we have sinned against God in thought or word or deed. Only in light of that gap between us and the kingdom's perspectives can we turn anew toward the kingdom with renewed commitment. Precisely in that positive, forward-looking sense did Lancelot Andrewes understand the turning involved in repentance: it means above all that we must 'look forward to God, and with our whole heart resolved to turn to Him'.[9] Confession of sin, understood as conversion, involves, then, a resolution to embrace the values of the kingdom which is to come. Such repentance is, in the words of one modern theologian, 'a return to the future'.[10]

So, the penitential prayer of the eucharist is part of our response to the Word of God expressed through the Scriptures. It arises out of encounter with the Word which provokes both judgement and hope.[11] It is an experience of 'the gladdening news of Judgement'[12] just as the dawning of the kingdom in our hearts and minds and imaginations is always cause of an acute sense of unworthiness and need as well as of joy and exultation. In so far as that is true for us we take another step toward the kingdom which is the goal of our eucharistic journey. For to see ourselves more clearly with the eyes of Christ – eyes perfectly focused on the kingdom's perspectives – is to become a little more like him.

Life has been given you for repentance, do not waste it on other things.

St Isaac the Syrian

The essence of all virtue is our Lord Jesus Christ.

St Maximus the Confessor

The mystery of the Kingdom of Heaven is that only the declaring, publishing, the notifying, and confessing of my sins possesses me of the Kingdom of Heaven.

John Donne

When man was fallen from his first estate, God opened to him a door of repentance, which he hath not vouchsafed to the Angels that fell, and so we crave God's favour, not only as we are the work of God's hands, but as we are his own image.

Lancelot Andrewes

Faith without repentance is not faith but presumption . . . repentance without faith is not repentance but despair.

Robert Sanderson

9

'The Voice of Eucharist':
Thanksgiving

To the loving-kindness of God made known in Jesus
Christ the response of intercession and penitence can
never be enough. As the great Swiss theologian Karl
Barth once insisted, the proper response to grace is
thanksgiving. 'Grace and gratitude', he said, 'belong
together like heaven and earth. Grace evokes gratitude
like the voice an echo. Gratitude follows grace like thun-
der lightning.'[1] Those sentiments take us straight to the
theme of this chapter, 'the voice of eucharist', as the
seventeenth-century divine Jeremy Taylor once put it.[2]
For now we consider our responsive prayer to God in the
principal prayer of the eucharist – 'the prayer', as our
Christian forebears often called it – the eucharistic
prayer or the great thanksgiving.[3]

Over the past fifty years or so much has happened to
re-establish the proper shape and content of this most
important prayer of the eucharist. As the Anglican
scholar Dom Gregory Dix so brilliantly showed, in and
around the great thanksgiving in its historic forms are
four basic acts: the taking, blessing, breaking and giving
of bread and wine.[4] In Anglican churches, as in others,
the modern thanksgiving prayers show a heightened
awareness of its special character.[5] We have come to
see the limitations of Archbishop Cranmer's eucharistic
prayer which was carried over from the 1552 to the 1662

editions of the *Book of Common Prayer*. We have modern-
ized the language and images of the prayers. In some
cases we have reclaimed ancient eucharistic prayers in
adapted forms, and we have added acclamations to
encourage congregational participation.[6] But how have
those changes affected our actual understanding and
experience of the great thanksgiving? More particularly,
have we come to appreciate better the place and the
possibilities of thanksgiving at the eucharist? Have we
become more adept at eucharistic praying?

Such questions may seem irrelevant at first sight.
After all, the great thanksgiving is unquestionably a
prayer prayed by the presiding bishop or priest. It has
been so almost from the beginning. It might seem, therefore, that the extent of the congregation's interest in it is
exhausted by attentive listening and solemn assent.[7]
Perhaps more significantly, though, most of us regard
this prayer chiefly as a prayer of consecration by which
the sacrament of Christ's Body and Blood is made present for us to share in. 'Silence falls. Awful words are
said. A bell rings. A miracle is accomplished.'[8] To be
sure, most Christians through the ages have believed in
the transformation of the bread and wine, however
differently they might express the mystery. But the
eucharistic prayer itself has not generally been understood only in terms of the consecration of the bread
and wine of communion. In the Anglican tradition, for
instance, it was only in the 1662 *Book of Common Prayer*
that it began to be described as a 'prayer of consecration'. Such a description focuses upon the effect of the
prayer rather than on the character of the prayer itself.[9]
Over time that has obscured our appreciation of the
kind of prayer it is. Yet our concern for the prayer-shape
of the eucharist demands that we consider just that
issue. So we must begin by recognizing that the great
thanksgiving is a Christian adaptation of a principal

genre of Jewish prayer, namely, the *berakah*, which we commonly render as 'thanksgiving prayer' or, using its Greek form, 'eucharistic prayer'. The prayer-shape of the eucharist leads us to a consideration of thanksgiving, because it is not merely one aspect of our responsive prayer to God, but the chief form of our human response to God's loving-kindness to us in Jesus Christ and the Spirit.

Eucharistic Praying

In our earlier discussion of the service of the Word it appeared that every act of proclamation included responsive appropriation and exultation. Those responses, together with the prayers of intercession and penitence in the properly responsive part of the eucharist all arise out of a sense of God acting on behalf of his people. Those 'wonderful deeds of God' were not abstract truths about divinity or mysticism or speculation but concrete experiences by means of which the Lord God showed his care and brought to pass his purposes. As that experience of God gave birth to its own distinctive spirituality, the thanksgiving prayer, or *berakah*, was integral to it.[10]

The thanksgiving prayer was not, however, a prayer expressing gratitude in the way we commonly understand; it was not merely saying 'thank you'. Rather, it was a proclamation of God's great deeds on behalf of his people. As a prayer its basic form was twofold: first, a blessing of God ('Blessed are you, Lord God . . .'); then a recounting of the specific acts for which God was being blessed.[11] This was the 'common thread' in Jewish spirituality in Jesus' time.[12] Therefore it is little wonder that his own prayer should be cast in terms so typical of Jewish thanksgiving prayer. Take, for instance, that moment of his spontaneous prayer (one of the few recorded instances) after the return of the seventy disciples: 'In that same hour he rejoiced in the Holy Spirit and said, "I thank thee, Father, Lord of heaven and earth, that thou hast hidden these things from the wise and understanding and revealed them to babes; yea, Father, such was thy gracious will"' (Luke 10.21 *RSV*; see also Matt. 11.25–6). Notice how Jesus' own prayer to the Father exhibits the essential features of thanksgiving or eucharistic prayer. He begins by thanking God – it could just as rightly have been translated 'I praise thee, Father'[13] – and then he recounts the deeds of God for which praise is offered. For Jesus, as for every other Jew, the *berakah* or blessing-thanksgiving was the pre-eminent response to God arising out of the acknowledgement of God's actions on behalf of his people.[14]

As Jesus prayed, so did the first Christians. Their thanksgiving prayer involved praising God the Father for what he had done 'for us and for our salvation' in Jesus Christ and the Holy Spirit. In a notable passage in Paul's Second Letter to the Corinthians, where he speaks of faith and its consequences in the lives of believers, he reveals how central to Christian prayer such thanksgiving is:

> Since we have the same spirit of faith as he had who wrote, 'I believed, and so I spoke,' we too believe, and so we speak, knowing that he who raised the Lord Jesus will raise us also with Jesus and bring us with you into his presence. For it is all for your sake, so that as grace extends to more and more people it may increase thanksgiving, to the glory of God. (2 Cor. 4.13–15 *RSV*)

That is but one expression of a theme which fills Paul's letters: the privilege of thanksgiving made possible through faith in Jesus Christ. Paul's message to his readers, both Jewish and Gentile, is that thanksgiving of the kind described above is the very hallmark of resurrection life. It is with thanksgiving above all that the church as the body of Christ is to 'overflow': 'whatever you do, in word or deed, do everything in the name of the Lord Jesus, giving thanks to God the Father through him' (Col. 3.17).[15]

All of this urges us to see the culmination of Christian prayer in thanksgiving to God as in the Jewish and early Christian *berakah*. Such 'praise and thanksgiving' (to use Cranmer's phrase) is not, therefore, merely one sort of prayer, as older manuals on prayer suggest. It is the chief expression of prayerful response to God toward which our human response to God's loving-kindness must move.

Voices of Eucharist

When we turn to the eucharist and its prayer-shape these remarks on Jewish thanksgiving prayer are important. We can see, for instance, how the progressive prayer response to the proclamation of the Word reaches its high point in the great thanksgiving or eucharistic prayer. Hence its description, already mentioned at the beginning of this chapter, as *the* prayer of Christian worship. But how are we to experience this eucharistic prayer? More precisely, how is it to be *our* prayer even as it is the church's prayer?

A clue may lie in the theme of thanksgiving itself. As we have seen, in Christian as in Jewish prayer thanksgiving takes the form of praising God for the deeds which he has done on behalf of his people. For Christians that praise is centred on what God the Father has done through Jesus Christ and the Spirit. In keeping with that, our modern eucharistic prayers, like the ancient Christian prayers they are inspired by, seek to express a comprehensive view of the basis for Christian thanksgiving. The boundaries of such prayers are enlarged to include more than the atoning sacrifice of Christ on Calvary which Cranmer's Prayer Book and other worship traditions used to focus upon almost exclusively.[16] Now such thanksgiving prayers often include thanksgiving for creation itself, for the prophets and forerunners of the Good News, and even for our future hope as inheritors of God's kingdom to come.[17]

The principle beneath this characteristic is of major importance: namely, that although Christian thanksgiving reaches its height in remembering before God the deeds he has done in Jesus Christ, Christians see those acts at the centre of a wider tapestry of God's involvement with the world. That involvement begins with creation and continues ceaselessly until, as the Orthodox liturgy puts it, God has 'endowed us with his heavenly kingdom'. All of that long history is, for the Christian, seen in its true perspective in the light of Jesus Christ's resurrection. In that light the paschal pattern of life, by which *we* enter into that history, becomes discernible.

For that reason the motive for thanksgiving is never a merely impersonal one. It is not a case of what Fr Bouyer once called 'disinterested praise'. However much the causes of praise may have to do with God's dealings (often in the past) with his people as a whole, on the crest of such praise is the reality of personal relationship between the one who praises and the God who is praised.[18] Even in the Jewish experience of thanksgiving to God for the liberation of Israel from slavery in Egypt the motive for thanksgiving is personalized or interiorized. Indeed, the Exodus came to be understood as the centre and pattern of the history of the whole people because it was at the same time the basis of the personal history of each and every man and woman. Parts of the Jewish Passover ritual, celebrated in the home, witness to this personal identification with the act or acts for which God is blessed and thanked:

> In every generation [says the head of the household] let each [person] look on himself as if he came forth from Egypt . . . It was not only our [ancestors] that the Holy One, blessed be he, redeemed, but us as well did he redeem along with them . . . Therefore, we are bound to thank, praise, laud, glorify, exalt and adore him who performed all these miracles for our [ancestors] and for us. He brought us forth from slavery to freedom, from darkness to joy, from mourning to holiday, from darkness to light, and from bondage to redemption.[19]

For the Christian too this 'voice of eucharist' is not just a formal expression of prayer uttered by the priest or bishop on behalf of the gathered body of Christ. It is not an impersonal prayer as an earlier liturgical sensibility might have put it.[20] How could it be? For the whole thrust of the Good News is that each believer must so give his life over to God that he becomes a place where the wonderful deeds of God are brought to pass in conformity with Christ. 'God wills always and everywhere to work the mystery of his incarnation,' St Maximus the Confessor once affirmed, pointing to the bond which links the life of each believer to that of Christ and to the whole people of God.[21] What is called for, then, is an integration of personal and collective thanksgiving according to the pattern we have already applied to other occasions of prayer within the eucharist. For at the great thanksgiving above all the president of the congregation images Christ as he speaks to his Father in thanksgiving and love on behalf of his body and bride, the church, gathered around him. As elsewhere, so here the president gathers all our disparate eucharistic prayers, focuses them in the work of Christ and the Spirit, and completes them when he joins them to his prayer and offers them all 'through Jesus Christ our Lord'.

But what of our own personal eucharistic prayers offered as the climax of our response to God's Word? As far as we know the eucharistic prayer has never included silence for such prayers as does collective praying. So how is our private prayer integrated into the collective prayer of the great thanksgiving? Clearly a different and more subtle integration is called for. Instead of employing a designated silent space for the offering of private eucharistic prayer, the integration of the private and the corporate must be achieved, I think, by a thanksgiving-oriented spirituality. Such a spirituality, rooted in St Paul's vision of Christian life as perpetual thanksgiving, needs to become the overall context or spiritual disposition in which the great thanksgiving is heard and prayed. That eucharistic prayer then becomes the centre-piece of a tremendously wide chorus of thanksgiving to which every member of the congregation contributes.

The Paschal Pattern

The spirituality of eucharistic praying thus involves an ever deepening sensitivity to the way in which the paschal pattern is at work in our lives. This moment of the eucharist seeks to elicit from us a response of sheer praise for the ways in which we discern God's loving and gracious presence in our lives. Whereas previous occasions of response made use of silence, and prompted a kind of prayerful introspection, now the spiritual tone is wholly different. All that has preceded looks forward to this uplifting of hearts in praise, blessing and exultation as we recall before God the marvellous deeds he has done. What the seventeenth-century Anglican preacher Mark Frank said of worship generally is especially appropriate for our response of thanksgiving: 'Our souls magnify the Lord, our spirits rejoice in God our Saviour; our memories recollect and call to mind his benefits and what he has done for us; our hearts evaporate into holy flames and ardent affections and desires after him as their only hope and joy.'[22] In his own words Frank was merely reiterating an insight of St Paul: joy and thanksgiving converge in an inseparable union (1 Thess. 5.16f.).

Coming, then, to offer our response of praise and thanksgiving to God in conjunction with the great thanksgiving of the whole church we concelebrate (as the Orthodox often say) with the presiding priest or bishop. Indeed, it is part of the royal priesthood of Christ shared with every believer through his or her baptism that a personal 'sacrifice of praise and thanksgiving' is offered together with the church's great thanksgiving. It expresses our participation in that perfect eucharistic prayer which is at the heart of Christ's soul.[23] 'Each person has been ordained priest of his own person', one of the church fathers once affirmed, 'to make his body a temple and his heart a pure altar.'[24] Our own eucharistic praying, joined to the eucharistic prayer of the church as a whole, is an expression of that personal priesthood.

The Eucharistic Person

With the response of the great thanksgiving the prayer-shape of the eucharist, centred on proclamation and response, is virtually complete. With this act of thanksgiving a more fundamental fulfilment occurs as well, one which does not so much concern the eucharist itself as humankind for whose salvation and joy the eucharist

exists. It has been said that our ability to give thanks, far
from being incidental to our human nature, is in fact
elemental to it. In the Fall we ceased to be eucharistic
persons.[25] But in Christ eucharistic prayer – praise and
thanksgiving – becomes possible again. More than that,
it can become the natural response to God's revelation
of himself. 'When man stands before the throne of God,'
it has been said,

*when he has fulfilled all that God has given him to fulfil,
when all sins are forgiven, all joy restored, then there is
nothing else for him to do but to give thanks. Eucharist is
the state of perfect man. Eucharist is the life of paradise.
Eucharist is the only full and real response of man to God's
creation, redemption and gift of heaven.*[26]

*I have told the glad news of deliverance in the great
congregation.*

Psalm 40

*But you are a chosen race, a royal priesthood, a holy nation,
God's own people, that you may declare the wonderful deeds
of him who called you out of darkness into his marvellous
light.*

The First Letter of Peter (*RSV*)

*Let the peace of Christ rule in your hearts, to which indeed
you were called in the one body. And be thankful. Let the
word of Christ dwell in you richly, as you teach and admon-
ish one another in all wisdom, and as you sing psalms and*

hymns and spiritual songs with thankfulness in your hearts to God.

The Letter to the Colossians (*RSV*)

Direct your mind to God in gratitude.

Dante, *Paradiso*

Prayer is a state of continual gratitude.

St John of Kronstadt

10

Home-coming

The following entry is recorded in the diary of a prominent Welsh Methodist of the eighteenth century:

> June 18th, 1735, being in secret prayer, I felt suddenly my heart melting within me like wax before the fire with love to God my Saviour; and also felt not only love, peace, etc., but longing to be dissolved, and to be with Christ; then was a cry within my inmost soul, which I was totally unacquainted with before, Abba Father! Abba Father! I could not help calling God my Father; I knew that I was his child, and that He loved me, and heard me. My soul being filled and satiated, crying "Tis enough, I am satisfied. Give me strength, and I will follow thee through fire and water.' I could say I was happy indeed! There was in me a well of water springing up to everlasting life (John 4.14). The love of God was shed abroad in my heart by the Holy Ghost (Rom. 5.5).[1]

Those words, revealing an intense experience of communion with God, illustrate a spiritual sensibility which has characterized Jesus' followers from the earliest days. We see it in the episode recorded by St John when Philip approaches Jesus and asks him: 'Show us the Father, and we will be satisfied' (John 14.8). For St John certainly, and for other New Testament writers as well, Jesus' showing the Father is at the centre of his life and mission. What Philip craved and what so many Christians through the ages have in some way experienced is the concern of this final chapter. As we reach the end of the eucharistic journey in the act of sacramental communion, we look to that divine Person in whom the journey of all spirits finds its goal and repose. St Augustine's much quoted words come to mind: 'You made us for yourself and our hearts find no peace until they rest in you'.[2] Now, therefore, we consider where the dialogue of prayer has brought us, to what end, into whose presence the proclamation of God's Word and our responsive prayers of intercession, penitence and thanksgiving have led us.

Going to the Father

St John is especially helpful since he more than the other evangelists sees the significance of Jesus in terms of a 'commerce' between heaven and earth. The theme of movement between heaven and earth, between God and humankind, seems to fascinate St John as we know from the story of Jesus and Nathaniel in the opening chapter of his Gospel. 'You will see heaven opened,' Jesus avows, 'and the angels of God ascending and descending upon the Son of Man' (John 1.51). At the centre of St John's great tableau of salvation is Jesus' coming from the Father and returning to him. The events of Jesus' last days, culminating on Calvary and the empty tomb, are the events which make good his claim to be the 'Way' to the Father.

It is noteworthy that, unlike the other Gospels, St John's has no record of the Last Supper itself, the basis of the Christian eucharist. Instead, he presents an extended interpretation of the meaning of the Last Supper and of Jesus' death which the supper itself, recorded in the other Gospels, seeks to explain. For St John the theme of Jesus' return to the Father is a central aspect of his understanding of Jesus' death as well as of the supper which interprets and commemorates that death.[3]

Other New Testament writers take up the idea of Jesus' going to the Father in their own terms. St Paul speaks of the crucifixion of Jesus as the decisive means by which hostility between God and humankind is broken down so that in his body Jesus might present us holy, blameless and irreproachable before God (Col. 1.21-2). The writer of the First Letter of John somewhat more directly explains to his readers Jesus' role as reconciler when he describes him as 'before the Father' (1 John 2.1). Both cases complement St John's picture of Jesus going to the Father by asserting our presence before God *through* and *in* Jesus Christ who is now and everlastingly before God in union with us his body.

The theme of believers' presence before God as the body of Christ is one which earlier chapters have explored. It was explained then as the basis of all Christian prayer. Why, then, is it necessary to return to that theme now? In our discussion of collective prayer I tried to draw out the trinitarian character of such prayer: it is offered *in* the power of the Spirit *through* Jesus Christ *to* God the Father. Michael Ramsey's theme of the praying Jesus was introduced because it points to the fact that we can only pray *with* or *through* the ever praying Jesus as members of his body; he makes possible our confident approach to God. In all of this Jesus points beyond himself to the Father whom he has come to make known. Christ is, to use Dietrich Bonhoeffer's apt word, the 'centre' between us and God, and as such he is not by and in himself the goal of the Christian spiritual journey.[4] As in St John's Gospel, so in Christian prayer generally Jesus directs us beyond himself.

Face to Face

There is, I admit, an ambiguity here. It arises from the
fact that Jesus is, as St Paul says, 'the image of the invisible God' (Col. 1.15). It means that we only know the
face of God in the face of Jesus of Nazareth. As a consequence we cannot adequately depict God; we can only
look upon Jesus in the belief that God is more like that
than like anything else. Christian art has wrestled with
this ambiguity but has not been able to resolve it. It
cannot, in fact, be resolved. Yet one of the most effective
means of stating both truths – that God is unseen, and
yet seen in Jesus Christ – has been attempted by Christian artists in the Orthodox tradition. A depiction common on old Slavonic crosses is an example. They show,
as most crosses do, the body of the crucified Jesus. But
then above the head of Christ is a veil suspended by
angelic hands on which is printed the face of Jesus. It
signifies God the Father. For as Jesus is the image of his
Father, so the Father, dwelling in light inaccessible, is
recognized in the face of his Son.

That same truth, conveyed by Christian art, is enacted
at the eucharist through the offering of the great thanksgiving and in receiving communion. Like the collect
prayer at the beginning, the eucharistic prayer is
addressed to God through Christ in the power of the
Spirit. The spiritual thrust of both acts is not toward
Christ but towards the God to whom he forever points.
Christ is the centre and the way but not in or by himself
the goal of our spiritual journey. As for Jesus, so for
us, the journey is a return to the Father. Our journey
Godward does not, therefore, end in making our communion by receiving Christ's sacramental body and
blood. Rather, it ends in our joyful presence before God
the Father, a presence made possible in a special way by
sacramental participation in Christ who is ever before

the Father. It may even be most appropriate to view the act of communion not as one in which we receive Christ but one in which he receives us. As he ever lives before the Father, so do we in a sacramental way at the climax of our eucharistic journey. 'Our communion is with the Father, and with his Son Jesus Christ our Lord' (1 John 2.1).

The Christian tradition has not always been unattuned to this insight. When, for instance, Archbishop Cranmer revised the eucharist for the English church in the sixteenth century he showed a keen sensitivity to this New Testament view of the direction of Christian prayer. One of his most notable changes was that he placed the Lord's Prayer immediately after the act of communion itself. Cranmer's precise motives for this change are not clear, but the overall message is: only when we are in Christ are we able – or 'bold', as the *Book of Common Prayer* used to say – to call God 'Father' as Jesus himself did. For Cranmer and the subsequent Prayer Book tradition the act of communion offered a special prerogative to communicants to call upon God as Jesus taught his followers to do. Only through Christ – here through sacramental participation in him – is our drawing near to God most fully possible. Whether or not the Lord's Prayer is said after communion, as Cranmer preferred, or before it as was more anciently done, is less important than appreciating the emphasis which the Lord's Prayer gives to the act of communion. The point which Cranmer's Communion Service sought to make is one which is true of every act of sacramental communion: it is the chief covenanted moment this side of heaven when our life 'in Christ' is expressed as life lived in the loving and forgiving presence of God.

Our Father

There is still more to be said about the Lord's Prayer and the climax of our eucharistic journey. Of course the Lord's Prayer contains much that is basic to all Christian prayer. As I said earlier its themes occur again and again in the Christian spiritual experience. Heaven, the divine name, kingdom, the divine will, the believer's daily bread – all of these themes, given to us by Jesus, echo throughout the Christian's life of prayer as the melody line of our song to the Lord.[5] But the theme of God as 'Father' stands as one of the most distinctive contributions of Jesus to our experience of God.[6] In so far as the eucharist is a journey of ever deepening communion in the prayer and experience of Jesus, we are bound to be drawn toward a climactic enunciation of Jesus' own form of address: 'Father in heaven'.

Jesus shared the distinctive awareness of his Jewish forebears that the God revealed in their history was not known first and foremost as a philosophical truth. Rather, he was known to them as the one who loved them and acted on their behalf. As the people of Israel experienced him, God was more like a person than like an impersonal agent or power. Jesus must have assumed this. But he went further still. For him God was personal; but God also had a name and a desire for intimacy of relationship which could only be likened – however inadequately – to the closeness of relationship between a loving father and a much loved child.

For a long time we have thought that Jesus' own expression, 'Abba', a child's term of intimacy, was uniquely his.[7] 'Abba' seems, in fact, to have denoted not merely a child's form of address to a parent but an address which combined deep love and intimacy with the sort of respect, even deference, which one adult might accord to another.[8] In any case, it surely betokened on

the lips of Jesus an intimacy and solidarity with God
which many of his contemporaries found disturbing or
even blasphemous.

And yet that very relationship of intimacy with the
Father was one which Jesus' disciples eagerly embraced
for themselves as something new and liberating. St Paul
provides vivid testimony to the impact of Jesus' sense of
God as Father among the first generation of Christians.
For Paul it is of a piece with the Good News of our incorporation into Christ. 'For', he explains to the Christians
in Rome,

> all who are led by God are children of God. For you
> did not receive a spirit of slavery to fall back into fear,
> but you have received a spirit of adoption. When we
> cry 'Abba! Father!' it is that very Spirit bearing witness
> with our spirit that we are children of God. (Rom.
> 8.14–16 *NRSV*)

Paul's words here, together with the overall testimony of
his writings, make clear that Christian spirituality
involves a wonderful and new sense of God as Father; a
spirituality of pilgrimage in which we are to progress
into a deeper sense of intimacy and communion with
God, an intimacy and communion betokened by the
word 'Abba'.

Church fathers too were insistent upon the importance of this scandalous intimacy with God the Father to
which Christians, unlike others, had access through their
participation in Christ by baptism and the eucharist. St
Irenaeus, for instance, writing in the second century,
wrote that God is '"Most High", "Almighty" and "Lord
of Hosts" to all people'; yet 'to the faithful only "He is
as a Father".' And more forcefully still he asserted:
'Behold, we speak with the Father and stand face to face
with Him.'[9]

When we turn to the early church's worship the

theme of the Father God recurs in the different eucharistic prayers. Justin Martyr, writing around the first half of the second century and recalling patterns already established, spoke of the president of the worship offering prayer 'glorifying the Father of all things through the name of the Son and of the Holy Spirit'.[10]

As time went on the character of the eucharistic prayers became more complex. They reflected the more sophisticated views of later generations of believers and sensitivity to newly formulated doctrines. Amid such developments the invocation of God as Father remained – the eucharist attributed to St Basil refers to Christ as the one who shows God as 'Father'[11] – but it lost some of the prominence which it clearly had in New Testament and early Christian prayer. The simple New Testament vision of the Christian life lived in the loving, attentive presence of the Father was expanded into a cosmic drama in which transcendence and mystery played an ever larger part.[12]

In the light of those developments it is interesting to find that in the fourth century, when those different characteristics were entering Christian worship, the Lord's Prayer was added to the eucharist. In his *Catechetical Lectures* to those newly baptized, Bishop Cyril of Jerusalem gave an exposition of the eucharist in which he comments: 'Then . . . we say that prayer which the Saviour handed down to his disciples, with a clear conscience addressing God as Father and saying "Our Father in heaven . . ."'.[13] Cyril emphasizes the particular Christian privilege of calling upon God as Father. Perhaps it was an attempt to maintain in Christian spirituality an awareness of access and intimacy with God when his otherness and mystery were being increasingly stressed.[14]

However that may be, in the sixteenth-century reformed liturgies such as that of the *Book of Common*

Prayer the theme reappeared as a consequence of the Reformers' return to a Bible-based spirituality. It was a chief benefit of their widely preached doctrine of justification by faith which stressed, among other things, that in Christ Christians should 'come boldly before the throne of grace' (Heb. 4.16) and enjoy a new access to God through Christ. In this there was a return to the biblical spirituality which they sought. Archbishop Cranmer took all this to heart when he composed the eucharistic prayer of the 1552 *Book of Common Prayer*. His eucharistic prayer, at the centre of which stands the Lord's Prayer, is litany-like in its calling upon God as Father. Consider the succession of invocations: 'our heavenly Father', 'O merciful Father', 'O Lord and heavenly Father', 'O Father Almighty'; and after the Lord's Prayer itself: 'O Lord and Heavenly Father', and 'O Father Almighty' in its emphatic, concluding phrase.

Anglican divines of the seventeenth century took Cranmer's point. 'Christ might have devised many more magnificent and excellent terms for God,' Lancelot Andrewes said, preaching on the specialness of the Christian invocation 'Our Father', 'but none were apt and fit for us, to assure us of God's favour.' And again, 'Christ teaching us to call God by the name of "Father", hath made choice of that word which might serve most to stir us up unto hope; for it is *Magnum nomen sub quo nemini desperandum*, 'a great name under which no man can despair'.' And for Andrewes, following St Cyprian fourteen centuries before, this privilege comes to us only in and through Christ: 'Who durst', saith Cyprian 'pray God by the name of Father, if Christ our advocate did not put these words in our mouths?'[15] There has been, then, a persistent awareness of the Christian's privilege of knowing God as Father. Whereas its basis is our baptismal union with Jesus Christ as members of his body, the church, its recurring expression and experience is in our holy communion with the exalted Christ as he stands before the Father in love, joy and thankfulness.

Admittedly, there are aspects of this emphasis which some people find difficult. Earlier in our century, for instance, the American theologian William Porcher DuBose noticed that the awareness of sonship in Christ is so much a part of a once Christian culture that we now view that intimate spiritual relationship with God as a fact quite apart from Christ. But no, he insisted. 'It is a truth in Jesus rather than in nature.'[16] In other words, it comes through the gift of God's Spirit and in no other way.

In recent years the issue of sexist language has raised questions about the appropriateness of this decidedly male language and imagery. For some it has proved to be a barrier. In an analysis of the reasons for not praying, the French theologian Jacques Ellul has invoked the psychological need for the death of the father. 'Haunted by words and images derived from a cheap Freudianism,' he wrote, 'we take it for granted that a child does not become a man until he has killed his father.'[17] From there it has been a short step to target the designation of God as Father as one of our society's most 'oppressive tendencies'.[18] But Christians should not readily jettison that form of address which Jesus himself used and encouraged. They may, however, wish to make it a more accessible form of address by complementing it with other notions which upbuild its possible meanings.

For instance, early on in Christian reflection on the experience of God, the notion of God as Father gave rise to speaking about God as 'person'. For one twentieth-century theologian, building upon that early tradition, the notion of God as 'infinite' or 'supreme Person'[19] signifies a way of life oriented toward and fulfilled *in communion with others*. Jesus, in revealing to us God as Father, has revealed to us the perfect community of

persons, the perfect communion of love which exists
between the Father, the Son and the Holy Spirit.[20] God
is personal in that he expresses himself in seeking communion and love with other divine and human persons.
For Jesus, God was Father because he was also the 'Thou'
whom he loved and with whom he had the deepest
union. So for us in Christ, God the Father, the personal
God, becomes a Thou, indeed our 'ultimate Thou'[21]
whom we love even as we are loved.

Behind this brief digression into theology lies a
tremendous depth of Christian meditation about God.
That reality will always elude our attempts to catch it in
precise words. Anyway, in the end, the eucharistic experience of God is not one which seeks to explain the
mystery in words. Instead it invites us into an experience
which includes but goes beyond the effort of the mind
and the power of discursive speech. And so, at the climax
of the eucharist, when we approach the divine Thou
through participation in the divine Son, we do not
expound a creed. Rather, we act out with the language
of our bodies, with sign and symbol, with celebratory
song, the joyful intimacy with the Father which is ours in
Christ.

The joy of this home-coming communicates itself in
different ways. I remember, for instance, a celebration
of the eucharist with a Coptic Christian from Egypt
present. He participated with expected decorum throughout the service, but when the time came to say the
Lord's Prayer he suddenly opened wide his arms with
palms upward in the traditional posture of Christian
prayer. It spoke more eloquently than any words could of
a deep joy, a simple desire to embrace the Father whom
he was now able to call upon and approach through
communion in Christ.

That sensibility seems to have characterized
Christians generally before the more creeping piety of

the Middle Ages so altered the tone of Christian eucharistic worship.[22] From evidence that remains it seems that the procession up to communion was up-beat and accompanied by the joyful singing of psalms by an exulting congregation. 'O taste and see that the Lord is good!' (Ps. 34.8) was one of the popular refrains. Although Cranmer was not wholly aware of those ancient practices when he revised the English Communion Service, he did nevertheless grasp that the event of communion was cause of great joy and praise. It is striking how his Communion Service builds toward a jubilant singing of the angels' chorus 'Glory be to God on high!' after the sacrament has been received. For sheer dramatic force and profound theological insight it is a pattern whose rationale, if not precise form, we would do well to reclaim. How else could we adequately reflect the delight of returning to him who satisfies all restless and journeying hearts?

In the act of communion our home-coming is accomplished. Not that we do it only once. The whole of life is a pattern of going and returning, of straying and coming home. Whereas we are prodigal, God our Father is constant in his love and ever welcoming when we respond to his call. Christians gather for the eucharist not once but again and again as if to express the Father's perennial call to us and hope for our return. Like the father in Jesus' parable our heavenly Father is always ready with a feast when we, his prodigal children, come home. And every home-coming is different, just as every embrace is. What remains the same is the limitless loving-kindness of the Father who is our alpha and omega, our beginning and our end.

Be Thou my vision, O Lord of my heart,
Be all else but naught to me, save that Thou art,
Be Thou my best thought in the day and the night,
Both waking and sleeping, thy presence be light.

Be Thou my wisdom, be Thou my true word
Be Thou ever with me, and I with Thee, Lord,
Be Thou my great Father, and I thy true son,
Be Thou in me dwelling, and I with Thee one.

Be Thou my breastplate, my sword for the fight,
Be Thou my whole armour, be Thou my true might,
Be Thou my soul's shelter, be Thou my strong tower,
O raise Thou me heavenward, great Power of my
*　　　　　　　　　　　　　power.*

Riches I heed not, nor man's empty praise,
Be Thou my inheritance now and always,
Be Thou and Thou only the first in my heart,
O Sovereign of heaven, my treasure Thou art.

High King of heaven, Thou heaven's bright Sun,
O grant me its joy after vict'ry is won,
Great Heart of my own heart, whatever befall,
Still be Thou my vision, O Ruler of all.

A Celtic Prayer

*

But let the praises of God, the hearing of His Scriptures read and expounded, the common prayers of the Church, and the celebration of the Eucharist, be performed with that discretion for the order, with that choice for the substance, with that reverence for the outward visage and fashion of what is said and done respectively at each of these parts of God's public service, and let me not doubt that God the author, and men strangers to our profession, should join in making good and acknowledging that of the Apostle, 1 Cor. xiv.25, that God is among us of a truth.

Herbert Thorndike,
The Service of God at Religious Assemblies (1641)

Notes

Introduction

1. James Sibbald, "'Holiness to the Lord'", in *The Funeral Sermons, Orations, Epitaphs, and Other Pieces on the Death of the Right Rev. Patrick Forbes, Bishop of Aberdeen* (Edinburgh, 1845), p. 153.

2. Metropolitan Anthony [Bloom], *Meditations on a Theme* (London: Mowbray, 1980), p. 46.

3. See, for instance, the historical studies of Josef Jungmann SJ, *The Early Liturgy to the Time of Gregory the Great* [Liturgical Studies, Vol. VI], Trans. Francis Brunner CSSR (Notre Dame, In.: University of Notre Dame Press, 1959 and London: Darton, Longman and Todd, 1960), and Willy Rordorff and others, *The Eucharist of the Early Christians*, trans. Matthew J. O'Connell (New York: Pueblo, 1970). Likewise, the practical pastoral discussions of Michael Perham, *Liturgy Pastoral and Parochial* (London: SPCK, 1970), and *Lively Sacrifice: The Eucharist in the Church of England Today* (London: SPCK, 1992) for the Church of England's *Alternative Service Book* (1980) and supplementary liturgical texts; and for the American *Book of Common Prayer* (1979) see Marion J. Hatchett, *Commentary on the American Prayer Book* (New York: Seabury Press, 1981) and Dennis G. Michno, *A Priest's Handbook: The Ceremonies of the Church*, Second Edition (Harrisburg, Pa.: Morehouse, 1983, 1986).

4. Jacques Ellul, *Prayer and Modern Man*, trans. C. Edward Hopkin (New York: Seabury Press, 1970), p. vi.

5. Alan W. Jones, *Journey into Christ* (Boston: Cowley, 1992), p. 1.

6. Bloom, *Meditations*, p.46.

Chapter 1. Beginning the Journey

1. Recounted by Kallistos Ware, *The Orthodox Way* (Crestwood, NY: St Vladimir's Seminary Press, 1979), p. 7. [London: Mowbray, 1979]

2. Thomas Traherne, *Christian Ethiks: or, Divine Morality, opening the way to blessedness by the rules of vertue and reason* (London, 1675), sig. A2 recto.

3. Alexander Schmemann, *For the Life of the World*, second edition (Crestwood, NY: St Vladimir's Seminary Press, 1973), p. 29.

4. Hans Urs von Balthasar, *Elucidations*, trans. John Riches (London: SPCK, 1975), p. 66.

5. Text from *The Alternative Service Book 1980*, p. 119; henceforth cited as *ASB*. See also the 1979 American *Book of Common Prayer* (cited as American *BCP*), p. 335.

Chapter 2. The Prayer-shape of the Liturgy

1. See Michael Ramsey, *Be Still and Know: A Study of the Life of Prayer* (London: Collins, in association with Faith Press, 1982), chapter one.

2. Ramsey, *Be Still and Know*, p. 20.

3. The Roman Catholic liturgist and theologian Louis Bouyer quotes the apposite comment of Pope Pius XI: 'Spiritually, we are all Semites'. See *History of Christian Spirituality*, Vol. I, *The Spirituality of the New Testament and the Fathers*, trans. Mary Perkins Ryan (New York: 1963), p. 3. [London: Burns and Oates, 1963]

4. This calling together of the people is called in Hebrew *qahal*, and in the New Testament *ecclesia*, 'congregation' or 'church'. See Louis Bouyer, *Introduction to Spirituality*, trans. Mary Perkins Ryan (Collegeville, Mn.: The Liturgical Press, 1961), p. 29. [London: Darton, Longman and Todd, 1963]

5. Psalm 136 is an especially good illustration of the way this basic pattern came to shape Hebrew–Jewish prayer. Each verse is divided between a proclamation of the word – in

fact a recounting of God's saving deeds for Israel – and a response by the congregation: 'For his mercy endures forever!'

Chapter 3. Collective Prayer

1. Evelyn Underhill, *Worship* (London: Nisbet, 1936), p. 278.
2. For the 'classic' collect form see Louis Weil, *Gathered to Pray: Understanding Liturgical Prayer* (Cambridge, Mass. and Cincinnati, Oh.: Cowley Publications/Forward Movement, 1986), pp. 43–4.
3. Seventeenth-century commentaries on the Anglican *Book of Common Prayer* made much of the collects as sources of meditation throughout each week and season.
4. Louis Bouyer uses the phrase; see his *Introduction*, p. 45.
5. See Weil, *Gathered*, p. 53. It is noteworthy that even in the seventeenth century English liturgical scholars were aware of the ancient combination of personal and corporate prayer within the framework of the collects at the eucharist. See, for instance, Anthony Sparrow's *A Rationale upon the Book of Common Prayer of the Church of England* (London, 1657), where he says that the congregation's petitions ('to wit, those that the people had then made before the Collect') preceded the collect said by the priest (p. 81).
6. See, for instance, the *ASB*, p. 119 and *passim*.
7. I have found useful here Enzo Bianchi, 'Contemporary Challenges to Prayer', *Concilium*, 3 (1990), pp. 45–59. The entire issue concerns the theme 'Asking and Thanking'.
8. Louis Bouyer, *Liturgical Piety* [Liturgical Studies, Vol. I] (Notre Dame, In.: University of Notre Dame Press, 1955), p. 17. Bouyer speaks of the 'inherent and mutual relation of the "subjective" and "objective" in piety', by which he means 'the mutuality existing between the person and the church'.
9. Bouyer, *Introduction*, pp. 43–4.
10. For the historical details see Weil, *Gathered*, pp. 34, 51–6.

11. By 'order' is meant the baptized laity, the episcopate, the presbyterate and the diaconate.

12. See Canon 19 of the Council of Laodicea. In describing the collective prayer pattern of the intercessions, the prayer act is presented as three acts: first, a bidding prayer for a particular intention ('Let us pray for . . .'); then, prayer offered 'silently' or 'hushed' [*dia siōpēs*]; and lastly, prayer offered by the president and 'spoken publicly' or 'aloud' [*dia prosphōneseōs*].

13. Bouyer, *Introduction*, p. 57.

14. Max Picard, *The World of Silence*, trans. Stanley Godman (London: Harvill, 1948), pp. 19, 40.

15. Picard, *World of Silence*, p. 36.

16. Picard, *World of Silence*, p. 27.

17. St Ignatius of Antioch, *Letter to the Ephesians*, xix, 1; text from Kirsopp Lake, ed., *The Apostolic Fathers*, I [Loeb Classical Library] (London: Heinemann, 1975), p. 192.

18. T. S. Eliot, *Burnt Norton*, from *The Four Quartets*, *The Complete Poems and Plays* (London: Faber and Faber, 1969), p. 175.

19. From his *Moralia in Job*, quoted by Aelred Squire, *Asking the Fathers* (London: SPCK, 1973), pp. 133–4.

20. Underhill, *Worship*, p. 271.

21. Bouyer, *Introduction*, p. 45.

22. The English word 'collect' now referring to a specific genre of liturgical prayer is derived from the Latin terms for such prayers, *collecta* and *collectio*.

23. As an aside, it seems to me that the relationship of silent prayer to vocal prayer is akin to that between private theological opinions, on the one hand, and the church's dogmatic tradition, on the other.

24. See, for instance, two modern aids to praying the collects: H. P. Finnis, *Meditations on the Sunday Collects* (London: SPCK, 1962), and J. W. C. Wand, *Reflections on the Collects* (London: A. R. Mowbray & Co., 1964). These books are based on the collects of the 1662 *Book of Common Prayer*, many of the collects from which can still be found in the revised Anglican service books. For a wholly contemporary treatment based on the collects of the American *BCP*

see Herbert O'Driscoll, *Prayers for the Breaking of Bread* (Cambridge, Mass. and Cincinnati, Oh.: Cowley Publications, 1991).

25. Michael Ramsey, *The Christian Priest Today* (London: SPCK, 1972), p. 13.

26. Ramsey, *Christian Priest*, pp. 13–14.

27. Josef Jungmann SJ, *The Place of Christ in Liturgical Prayer*, trans. A. Peeler (London: Geoffrey Chapman, 1965), p. 146.

28. Baldassare da Valdiporro, 'La Preghiera e il Nome di Gesù in San Giovanni', *Studia Patavina*, 2 (1961), pp. 196–7.

29. Josef Jungmann SJ, *Liturgy of the Word*, trans. H. E. Winstone (London: Burns and Oates, 1966), p. 72.

30. This theme is discussed in Arthur Michael Ramsey, *The Gospel and the Catholic Church*, second edition (London: Longmans, Green & Co., 1956), pp. 143–4, where he alludes, for instance, to Athanasius, *Contra Arianos*, II, 12.

31. Athanasius, *Contra Arianos*, I, 41.

32. '*Totus Christus, caput et corpus.*' The theme together with many citations in Augustine's writings is discussed by Antonio Piolanti, 'Il mistero del "Cristo totale" in S. Agostino' in the collection *Augustinus Magister* [Congrés International Augustinien] (Paris, 1954), II, pp. 453–69.

33. Richard Hooker, *The Laws of Ecclesiastical Polity*, Book V, lvi. 7 (Oxford, 1841 [Keble Edition]), II, p. 249.

34. The arrangement is described thus by Louis Bouyer in his essay 'Bishops in the Church: The Catholic Tradition' in Peter Moore, ed., *Bishops: But What Kind?* (London: SPCK, 1982), pp. 27–8.

35. Jungmann, *Liturgy of the Word*, p. 65.

36. In light of this conjunction of head and body it is wrong to assert that the bishop or priest who presides at the eucharist represents *either* Christ *or* the people. It is more accurate to say that the celebrant presents – makes present symbolically – Christ *as head*, and that the gathered assembly presents Christ *as body*.

Chapter 4. The Mystery of the Word: Proclamation

1. See Hans Urs von Balthasar, *Prayer*, trans. A. V. Littledale (New York: 1961), p. 39. [London: Geoffrey Chapman, 1961]
2. *In Cant.* I. I (*Patrologia Latina* [henceforth cited as *PL*] 172: 359).
3. See Andrew Louth, *Discerning the Mystery: An Essay on the Nature of Theology* (Oxford: Clarendon Press, 1983), p. 101.
4. Robert E. Terwilliger, *Receiving the Word of God* (New York: 1960), p. 71. [London: A. R. Mowbray and Co., 1961]
5. Terwilliger, *Receiving*, p. 72.
6. David Holeton, 'The Sacramental Language of S. Leo the Great', *Ephemerides Liturgicae*, XCII (1978), p. 162.
7. Herbert Thorndike, *The Laws of the Church* in *Theological Works* IV (Oxford, 1853), p. 917.
8. The pattern is repeated in an adapted form in 2 Kings 23 and Nehemiah 8 according to Bouyer, *Introduction*, pp. 28–31; see the discussion above, p. 13.
9. Again, see Luke 16.14–21.
10. Bouyer, *Introduction*, p. 40.
11. See the form as it is found in the American *BCP* service for Easter Eve, pp. 288–91, and in the English *Lent, Holy Week and Easter: Services and Prayers* (London: Church House, 1986), pp. 243–70.
12. Romano Guardini, *Before Mass*, trans. E. C. Briefs (London: Longmans, Green and Co., 1957), pp. 11–12.
13. Guardini, *Before Mass*, p. 12.

Chapter 5. '*Ephphatha!* Be Open!': Appropriation

1. Bouyer, *Introduction*, p. 27.
2. 'Tales of the Hasidim', in Buber, *The Early Masters* (New York: Schocken Books, 1975), p. 55. [London: Thames and Hudson, 1956]
3. Bouyer, *Introduction*, p. 53.
4. Gerard Hughes, *God of Surprises* (London: Darton, Longman and Todd, 1985), p. 33.

5. *How to Read the Bible* (Sketis, Egypt, n.d.), p. 23.

6. *Allegoria* is the usual Latin word for the deeper meaning of Scripture used by the Latin fathers from the fourth century onwards. The Antiochene fathers called allegory the 'contemplative meaning' (Louth, *Discerning*, p. 96).

7. See Benedicta Ward, *The Wisdom of the Desert Fathers* (Oxford: SLG Press, 1975), pp. xiii–xiv.

8. Ward, *Desert Fathers*, p. xiii.

9. Susan Muto, *Steps Along the Way: The Path of Spiritual Reading* (Denville, NJ: Dimension Books, 1975), p. 28.

10. Muto, *Steps*, p. 30; and more generally, pp. 82–107.

11. Muto, pp. 82–107.

12. See, for instance, the note on 'Silence' in the *ASB*, p. 117, and the rubrics in the American *BCP*, p. 357.

13. On the challenges of silence see Bloom, *Meditations*, pp. 16–17.

14. George Steiner comments, more generally, thus: 'The private reader or listener can become an executant of felt meaning when he learns the poem or the musical passage by heart. To learn by heart is to afford a text or music an indwelling clarity and life-force' (*Real Presences* [London: Faber, 1989], p. 9).

15. On this aspect of spiritual discipline flowing from *lectio* see Adrian van Kaam, *In Search of Spiritual Identity* (Denville, NJ: Dimension Books, 1975), pp. 84–5.

16. Hughes, *Surprises*, p. 46; for expanded practical comments on this type of prayer see pp. 40–54.

17. Quoted by Hughes, *Surprises*, p. 53.

18. Bouyer, *Introduction*, p. 34.

19. *Ambigua* (*Patrologia Graeca* [henceforth cited as *PG*] 91: 1084D).

20. Aidan Kavanaugh, *Elements of Rite. A Handbook of Liturgical Style* (New York: Pueblo, 1982), p. 27.

21. Thomas K. Carroll, *Preaching the Word* [Message of the Fathers to the Churches, Vol. 11], (Wilmington, Del.: Michael Glazier, 1984), p. 17.

22. John Donne, *Sermons*, eds. G. R. Potter and E. M. Simpson (Berkeley, CA: University of California Press, 1953–1962), vol. 6, p. 282; italics mine.

23. A vivid example of the fathers' unitive view of word and sacrament can be seen in the sermons of St Leo, treated by David Holeton in his article already cited (chapter four, note 6).

Chapter 6. 'He Who Sings Prays Twice': Exultation

1. Quoted by Ivor Jones, *Music: A Joy Forever* (London: Epworth, 1989), p. 70.
2. E.g. Luke 1.46–55, 68–79, 2.14, 29–32; Phil. 2.6–11; Rev. 4.8–11.
3. Jungmann, *Liturgy*, pp. 46–7.
4. See chapter four, note 11.
5. Kavanaugh, *Elements of Rite*, p. 31.
6. I follow the exposition of Jones, *Music*, p. 72.
7. Bouyer, *Introduction*, p. 42.
8. See the *Laws*, Book V, xxviii.3 [Keble ed., II, pp. 161–2]; and Thorndike's *Laws*, XXII, 30 in *Works*, IV, pp. 540–1.
9. Quoted by A. M. Allchin, 'The *Book of Common Prayer* and the Continuity of Tradition' in *The Kingdom of Love and Knowledge* (London: Darton, Longman and Todd, 1979), p. 123.
10. Jones, *Music*, pp. 71–2.
11. John Wesley, in the Preface to *A Collection of Hymns for Use of the People Called Methodists* (1779).
12. Wesley, Preface to *Hymns*.
13. Bouyer, *Introduction*, p. 42.
14. This connection was emphasized by Anglican commentators such as Charles Wheatley who wrote in *A Rational Illustration of the Book of Common Prayer* (London, 1710): 'And since in this Sacrament we are to renew our baptismal vow, (one branch of which was, that we should *believe all the articles of the Christian faith,*) it is very requisite that, before we be admitted [viz. to communion], we should declare that we stand firm in the belief of these articles' (Oxford [1846], p. 202).
15. Text as found in the American *BCP* (1979), p. 304; see also the English *ASB*, p. 245.

16. So Dionysius describes it in his work *The Ecclesiastical Hierarchy*, chapter 3; text from Colm Luibhead and Paul Rorem, eds. and trans., *Pseudo-Dionysius: The Complete Works* (London: SPCK, 1987 [Classics of Western Spirituality]), pp. 217–18. See as well Anthony Sparrow, *Rationale or Practical Exposition of the Book of Common Prayer* (London, 1659), p. 200.

17. From his work *The Church's Mystagogy*. Text in George C. Berthold, ed. and trans., *Maximus the Confessor. Selected Writings* (London: SPCK, 1985 [Classics of Western Spirituality]), p. 207.

18. *Maximus*, p. 207.

19. He comments thus on the Apostles' Creed, but his point applies to the Nicene Creed as well (Nicholas Ayo CSC, *The Creed As Symbol* [Notre Dame, In.: University of Notre Dame Press, 1989], pp. 2–3).

Chapter 7. For the Life of the World: Intercession

1. Kenneth Stevenson, 'And Ye shall Pray . . .' in Kenneth Stevenson, ed., *Liturgy Reshaped* (London: SPCK, 1982), p. 47.

2. Text as in Rordorff, *Eucharist*, p. 73.

3. Stevenson, *Liturgy*, p. 41.

4. Ramsey, *Be Still*, p. 41.

5. The prayer, originally from the sacramentary attributed to Pope Gelasius I, is found in the American *BCP*, p. 528.

6. J. Llopis, 'Is There Prayer in the Eucharist?', *Concilium*, 3 (1990), p. 85.

7. Schmemann, *Life*, pp. 27, 44.

8. The pattern is seen in its integrity in the so-called Solemn Collects of Good Friday; see, for instance, the American *BCP*, pp. 278–9 and the English *Lent, Holy Week and Easter*, pp. 212–16.

9. For this meaning of the Greek word *entugchanein* (translated as 'intercede' see B. F. Westcott, *The Epistle to the Hebrews*, reprinted (Grand Rapids, Mi.: Eerdmans, 1977), p. 191.

10. Andrew Murray, *The Ministry of Intercessory Prayer*, edited edition (Minneapolis, Minn.: Bethany House, 1981), p. 37.
11. Schmemann, *Life*, p. 44.
12. Ramsey, *Christian Priest*, p. 16.

Chapter 8. The Kingdom of Conversion: Penitence

1. Text from *St Athanasius: Selected Works and Letters*, in *Nicean and Post-Nicean Fathers*, vol. IV, eds. H. Ware and Philip Shaff (Oxford, 1892), p. 196.
2. On Augustine, at least, see Benedicta Ward, *Harlots of the Desert. A Study of Repentance in Early Monastic Sources* (Oxford: Mowbray, 1987), p. 5.
3. See the American *BCP* (1979), pp. 319, 351; and the English *ASB*, p. 120.
4. Wheatley, *Rational Illustration*, p. 99.
5. Wheatley, *Rational Illustration*, p. 99.
6. As, for instance, in the American *BCP* (1979), p. 360 and in the English *ASB*, p. 117, note 21.
7. In this interpretation of the iconographic tradition I follow Leonid Ouspensky, *Theology of the Icon* (Crestwood, NY: St Vladimir's Seminary Press, 1978), pp. 224–8.
8. For the phrase see Oliver O'Donovan, *Resurrection and Moral Order* (Leicester/Grand Rapids, Mi.: IVP and Eerdmans, 1978), p. 14.
9. Lancelot Andrewes, *Works*, vol. I. [Location of source unidentified.]
10. Jürgen Moltmann, *Theology and Joy*, trans. R. Ulrich (London: SCM, 1973), p. 63.
11. Bloom, *Meditations*, p. 116.
12. Bloom, *Meditations*, p. 2.

Chapter 9. 'The Voice of Eucharist': Thanksgiving

1. Karl Barth, *Church Dogmatics*, vol. IV, pt. I (Edinburgh: T. and T. Clark, 1956), p. 41.
2. The phrase is from the Dedication of *The Great Exemplar*

of *Sanctity and Holy Life* in Charles Page Eden, ed., *The Whole Works of The Right Rev. Jeremy Taylor, D.D.* (London, 1850), vol.2, p. 3.

3. See, for instance, the variety of prayers in the English *ASB*, pp. 130–41 and the American *BCP* (1979), pp. 361–3, 367–75.

4. See his discussion in 'The "Four-Action" Shape of the Eucharist' in *The Shape of the Liturgy*, second edition (London: Dacre Press, 1982), pp. 48–50.

5. A discussion of these new sensibilities can be found in Louis Bouyer, *Eucharist* (Notre Dame, In.: University of Notre Dame Press, 1968), *passim*.

6. In the English *ASB* the acclamations in the four eucharistic prayers are the same; in the American *BCP* (1979) they vary from prayer to prayer. See above, note 3.

7. The great thanksgiving, in whatever form, is customarily concluded by the 'Great Amen'. It is the chief response of ratification ('Amen' means 'so be it!') which the congregation says at the eucharist.

8. So Evelyn Underhill describes the atmosphere in *The Mystery of Sacrifice* (Harrisburg, Pa.: Morehouse, 1991), p. 41. [London: Longman and Co., 1938]

9. The prayer has been known variously as *eucharistia*, *anaphora*, *oration*, *prex*, *praedicatio* and *praefatio*. How in this pattern do we understand the eucharistic prayer as one of *consecration*? Does this schema not reverse the direction of the divine–human encounter at this point in the eucharist, namely, that the eucharistic prayer embodies and effects God's initiative in sanctifying the bread and the wine? In a sense, yes. But the sanctifying act of God, while still remaining God's act, can also be seen as God's responsive 'Amen!' (a covenanted response) to our sacrifice of praise and thanksgiving. In so far as that prayer expresses our response to God's Word to us it is a response to *his* initiative to make us his through communion. Once God has spoken his Word of invitation in the first part of the liturgy, and once we have responded with thanksgiving and 'Amen!', then God makes actual what his Word invites us to as promise and hope: communion with him through our incorporation into Christ by

the Holy Spirit. Thus this focus on the responsive character of the eucharistic prayer need not contradict the other complementary effect of the prayer, namely, the sanctification of the bread and wine.

10. On this prayer *genre* see Lawrence A. Hoffman, 'Rabbinic *Berakhah* and Jewish Spirituality', *Concilium*, 3 (1990), pp. 18–29.

11. See Psalm 136 for a vivid expression of this awareness.

12. Bouyer, *Eucharist*, p. 30.

13. The Greek word *exomologeisthai* means 'to praise' and is here translated in terms of the praise associated with Jewish thanksgiving. For another example see Luke 17.11–19.

14. Hoffman, '*Berakhah*', p. 18.

15. That is especially the theme of the Letter to the Colossians; see N. T. Wright, *The Epistles of Paul to the Colossians and Philemon* (Leicester/Grand Rapids, Mi.: IVP and Eerdmans, 1986).

16. This expanded notion of thanksgiving in the revised services of the eucharist is modelled on ancient Christian eucharistic prayers. It is worth noting, though, that the desire to recapture the early Christians' sense of the wide scope of thanksgiving in the eucharistic prayer goes back to the seventeenth century at least. Herbert Thorndike, for instance, argued that the eucharistic prayer in the *Book of Common Prayer* should recover that wide scope. See his treatise *Of Religious Assemblies* in *Theological Works*, I, i, pp. 337–41.

17. See, for instance, the American *BCP*, p. 369.

18. Bouyer, *Eucharist*, p. 30.

19. Quoted by Leonel Mitchell, *Praying Shapes Believing: A Theological Commentary on the Book of Common Prayer* (Harrisburg, Pa.: Morehouse, 1990), p. 163

20. See, for instance, Harton, *Elements*, pp. 288–9.

21. See chapter five, note 19.

22. *Sermons*, vol. II pp. 123–4.

23. Bouyer, *Eucharist*, p. 93. In explaining the significance of Jesus' prayer in Matt. 11.25–7 and Luke 10.21–2 Bouyer comments that 'this communication is but a radiation of the permanent "eucharist" which is at the very root of the soul of Christ.'

24. So comments Isadore of Pelusium in *Letter 75* to Bishop Theodosius (*PG* 78:784).
25. On this theme see Kallistos Ware, 'The Mystery of the Human Person', *Sobornost/ECR*, 3 (1, 1981), pp. 62–9.
26. Schmemann, *Life*, pp. 37–8.

Chapter 10. Home-coming

1. Quoted in A. M. Allchin and Esther de Waal, eds., *Threshold of Light: Prayers and Praises from the Celtic Tradition* (London: Darton, Longman and Todd, 1986), p. 29.
2. R. S. Pine-Coffin, trans., *The Confessions* (London: Penguin Books, 1961), Bk. I.1, p. 21.
3. For an interesting interpretation of the fourth Gospel as a kind of liturgy see Gordon Wakefield, *The Liturgy of St John* (London: Epworth, 1985).
4. Dietrich Bonhoeffer, *Christ the Center*, trans. Edwin H. Robertson (New York, 1966), p. 60. [*Lectures on Christology* (London: Collins, 1966), p. 60]
5. See chapter two, note 2.
6. So Joachim Jeremias has contended in *The Prayers of Jesus* (London: SCM Press, 1967).
7. So Jeremias, who has had a wide influence among New Testament scholars.
8. For an important qualification to Jeremias' interpretation see James Barr '"Abba, Father" and the Familiarity of Jesus' Speech', *Theology*, vol. XCI, no. 741 (May, 1988), pp. 173–9.
9. St Irenaeus, *Proof of the Apostolic Preaching*, trans. J. P. Smith in *Ancient Christian Writers*, vol. 16 (Westminster, Maryland/London, 1952), §8, p. 52; and again §96, p. 106.
10. *First Apology*, 65, 3; text quoted from Maurice Jourjon's essay on Justin in Rordorff, *Eucharist*, p. 72.
11. This liturgy of the eucharist is based upon worship traditions of the church in Cappadocia where St Basil was a bishop in the middle of the fourth century.

12. On the stress on transcendence beginning in fourth-century worship see J. G. Davies, 'The Introduction of the Numinous into the Liturgy: An Historical Note', *Studia Liturgica*, vol. 8 (1971/2), pp. 216–23.

13. Lecture 5, 11; text in Frank Cross, ed., *St Cyril of Jerusalem's Lectures on the Christian Sacraments: The Procatechesis and the Five Mystagogical Catecheses* (London: SPCK, 1966), p. 75.

14. It is notable too that the Lord's Prayer was part of the so-called 'discipline of secrecy' in which essential aspects of Christian belief and practice were kept secret from non-believers.

15. Sermon Seven in *Nineteen Sermons upon Prayer in General and the Lord's Prayer in Particular* in *Works*, vol. V, pp. 364–5.

16. William Porcher DuBose, *The Gospel in the Gospels*, second edition (London: Longmans, Green and Co., 1911), pp. 46–7.

17. Ellul, *Prayer*, p. 92.

18. Quoted by William Oddie, *What Will Happen to God? Feminism and the Reconstruction of Christian Belief* (London: SPCK, 1986), p. 12.

19. Dumitru Staniloae, *Teologia Dogmatică Ortodoxă*, 3 vols. (Bucureşti: Editura Institutului Biblic şi de Misiune, 1978), vol. I, pp. 78, 300–4. Translations my own.

20. For a fuller and more complex presentation of this theme see Fr Staniloae's essay 'The Holy Trinity: Structure of Supreme Love' in *Theology and the Church*, trans. Robert Barringer (Crestwood, NY: St Vladimir's Seminary Press, 1980), pp. 73–108.

21. So Hans Urs von Balthasar, 'The marian principle' in *Elucidations*, p. 66.

22. The radical changes in the ethos of eucharistic worship since the New Testament period are analysed by Nathan Mitchell, OSB, *Cult and Controversy: The Worship of the Eucharist Outside Mass* (New York: Pueblo, 1982).

Select Index

Index of
Biblical References